"This book is like opening a fror
living room of a significant perso:
will feel like the main characters a
sit spellbound at their Spirit-insp
Bi

"I am so encouraged and humbled by the stories of these remarkable men and women who responded in faith to the Holy Spirit's call on their lives and changed the world. Their lives are a testimony of what God can do with us if we step forward in faith and say yes to Him."

Samuel Rodriguez, president, National
Hispanic Christian Leadership Conference

"Dean Merrill knows that history is fundamentally a story, and he tells many engaging ones about some of the most extraordinary men and women of the last 120 years. They rightly fall under the heading 'Pentecostal,' yet they are people whose lives will impress Christians of any persuasion."

Mark Galli, former editor in chief, *Christianity Today*

"Church history is filled with the amazing narrative of God's grace and power working in and through human jars of clay. Dean Merrill has captured fifty of these incredible stories to remind us all of the potential within us when given to the Potter."

Tammy Dunahoo, vice-president, The Foursquare Church

"Pentecostals and charismatics are a younger Christian family that has grown rapidly and been all too often misunderstood and ste-reotyped. Dean Merrill offers fifty windows into this movement that increasingly represents what global Christianity is becoming in the twenty-first century: ordinary people hungry for God and empowered by His Spirit."

Byron D. Klaus, former president,
Assemblies of God Theological Seminary

"I was thrilled when I heard about Dean Merrill's book, *50 Pentecostal and Charismatic Leaders Every Christian Should Know*. This book creates a vital bridge to our past. I plan to share it with the young leaders I am discipling. My prayer is that the same fire of the Spirit that burned in the hearts of these legendary heroes of the faith will be rekindled in these challenging days."

J. Lee Grady, former editor, *Charisma*;
author, *Set My Heart on Fire*

"Through diligent research and gifted writing, Dean Merrill invites us on a journey alongside a diverse group of Spirit-empowered leaders, who are amazingly gifted and humanly flawed yet tremendously inspiring. You'll want to move beyond the bus station's ticket counter for further exploration with intense longing for the Spirit's miraculous demonstration in our generation."

Kay Horner, executive director, Pentecostal Charismatic
Churches of North America (PCCNA)

"Dean Merrill reminds us how our Lord uses women and men from various ethnicities, personalities and backgrounds to have Kingdom impact in their time through the Spirit's empowerment. This book stirred up my calling as a Pentecostal leader and motivated me to trust the Lord for gifts of faith in my own life."

David R. Wells, president, PCCNA;
vice chair, Pentecostal World Fellowship;
general superintendent, Pentecostal Assemblies
of Canada

"The vast number of Pentecostal and charismatic leaders who have played a role in the spread of these movements is often confusing. We are indebted to Dean Merrill for his judicious selection of key players. His short biographical sketches are clearly written and to the point. This volume should be a primer for anyone who wishes to learn about those who have contributed so much to the spread of the Pentecostal message. God is very much alive and acting through His Spirit throughout the world in ways fully consistent with the experience of the earliest Christians."

Cecil M. Robeck Jr., senior professor of Church history
and ecumenics, Fuller Theological Seminary

"Dean Merrill captures with exquisite clarity the diverse lives and multiple perspectives that shaped the Pentecostal and charismatic streams. Merrill reveals how encounters of the Spirit of God impacted imperfect people wrestling with racism, sexism, regionalism and differing viewpoints on war. A must read for students and scholars alike."

Daniel McNaughton, Ph.D., professor of practical theology,
Southeastern University

50 Pentecostal and Charismatic Leaders
Every Christian Should Know

50 PENTECOSTAL AND CHARISMATIC LEADERS
Every Christian Should Know

DEAN MERRILL

Chosen
a division of Baker Publishing Group
Minneapolis, Minnesota

Published by Chosen Books
11400 Hampshire Avenue South
Bloomington, Minnesota 55438
www.chosenbooks.com

Chosen Books is a division of
Baker Publishing Group, Grand Rapids, Michigan

Printed in the United States of America

Library of Congress Cataloging-in-Publication Data
Names: Merrill, Dean, author.
Title: 50 Pentecostal and charismatic leaders every Christian should know / Dean Merrill.
Other titles: Fifty Pentecostal and charismatic leaders every Christian should know
Description: Minneapolis, Minnesota : Chosen, a division of Baker Publishing Group, [2021]
Identifiers: LCCN 2020044496 | ISBN 9780800762025 (trade paperback) | ISBN 9780800761868 (casebound) | ISBN 9781493429813 (ebook)
Subjects: LCSH: Pentecostals—Biography. | Pentecostalism.
Classification: LCC BX8762.Z8 A315 2021 | DDC 269/.40922—dc23
LC record available at https://lccn.loc.gov/2020044496

Unless otherwise indicated, Scripture quotations are from THE HOLY BIBLE, NEW INTERNATIONAL VERSION®, NIV® Copyright © 1973, 1978, 1984, 2011 by Biblica, Inc.® Used by permission. All rights reserved worldwide.

Scripture quotations labeled AMP are from the Amplified® Bible (AMP), copyright © 2015 by The Lockman Foundation. Used by permission. www.Lockman.org

Scripture quotations labeled KJV are from the King James Version of the Bible.

Cover design by LOOK Design Studio
Cover photo of Wonsuk Ma © Oral Roberts University. Used by permission.

Cover photo of Aimee Semple McPherson by Los Angeles Public Library/Security Pacific National Bank Collection /Tibbals Studio—Los Angeles Public Library Photo Collection; File number: LAPL00024641, PD-US

Author is represented by Wolgemuth & Associates.

21 22 23 24 25 26 27   7 6 5 4 3 2 1

Contents

Foreword

It is my great privilege to write the foreword for this timely book. Dean Merrill has a special gift for combining valuable content with an engaging style, making learning both enjoyable and edifying. And edifying this book is, reminding us of the difference that empowerment by God's Spirit can make in our lives!

One mark of an ingeniously designed work is that it meets a need that its predecessors had not yet recognized. There are an increasing number of works on Pentecostal and charismatic history, and some biographical treatments of key figures. But where does one start? This book offers a handy primer on most of the leading figures—a valuable refresher for those schooled in Pentecostalism and a crucial survey to initiate beginners.

Pentecostals and charismatics will relish the book for treating some of their favorite figures and for filling gaps in knowledge about the histories of their movements. And outsiders will find this book valuable to expose them to the basics of the history and figures in a movement that is now exploding across the world. Depending on how one defines Pentecostals and charismatics, estimates of their global presence now often exceed half a billion, making them the second-largest Christian movement in the world after Roman Catholicism (which itself includes a substantial number of charismatics).

Understanding the development of Pentecostal and charismatic history, therefore, is valuable for every reader, and encountering stories about the lives of key figures is one of the most interesting ways to engage that history. Tracing these stories makes for exciting reading, especially at the hands of a nimble writer such as Dean Merrill. Even in our age of tweets and sound bites, and even for ADHD persons such as myself, this collection of fifty fast-moving, brief vignettes holds our attention.

With our respective interests and traditions, various readers might have added some different figures and left others out. Some would have included Charles Parham; I would have voted for Pandita Ramabai and (here my New Testament scholar bias is showing) Gordon Fee, while omitting a few figures, the naming of whom would further reveal my biases. In many cases, however, the figures we would have left out are those about whom we have the most to learn, and we already know enough about the figures we would have added. For the most part, the author's selections are ideal in providing a fairly representative cross-sample of Western charismatics and Pentecostals, especially from the past eighty years.

At this distance from the beginning of the Pentecostal revival, it is easier to identify the most influential figures than it might have been in the immediate wake of the initial revival. William Seymour's stature has rightly grown, for example, along with renewed appreciation of his impact. Because history requires some hindsight, it is more difficult to choose the most influential figures of the past half century. The charismatic movement, moreover, is diffuse, spread throughout so many denominations and sub-movements that few of us are familiar with all its reaches. This makes a primer on many of these figures all the more valuable. Recent figures are naturally also more controversial, but love them or hate them—hopefully in a Christian way!—they are figures and voices we should know.

Those concerned about any of the choices (or wondering why their pastor is left out!) should remember that these are inevitably samples. Yet Merrill has done a superb job in providing an array that reflects the great diversity of Pentecostals and charismatics: both genders, multiple ethnicities and representatives from a wide range of denominations. Because many of the selected figures were associated with other Pentecostal or charismatic leaders, moreover, Merrill manages to sneak in a few more figures than the fifty specifically named (for example, Carrie Judd Montgomery and Elias Letwaba) without adding extra space.

Much more remains to be said about significant figures in the history of Pentecostals and charismatics in Africa, Asia and Latin America than was possible in this book's limit of fifty. Historians will also say more about the figures included. The genius of this book, however, is what makes it invaluable for its purpose—as a handy, succinct and inexpensive gold mine of knowledge.

The stories in this book remind us that God uses all kinds of people, including people like us. All had flaws. As Merrill's balanced presentation of these figures points out, none was perfect. But God is eager to use those who recognize their need to depend on Him. This book reminds us of a God who calls to us all, ready to use any vessel wholly devoted to His service.

Dr. Craig S. Keener, F. M. and Ada Thompson Professor of
Biblical Studies, Asbury Theological Seminary

Introduction

Great Cloud of Witnesses

Some of the names in the table of contents you will quickly recognize, while others may be quite unfamiliar to you. But all of them (listed chronologically by order of birth) have stories to tell and insights to share out of the Pentecostal and charismatic movements of the past 120 years. In the words of esteemed Emory University professor Fred Craddock, "Anyone who can't remember further back than his or her own birth is an orphan."

Choosing the fifty was a challenge, to be sure, which involved long discussions with the publisher. You may see a name that causes you to say, "Why would you include *him*?" On the other hand, you may be asking, "How could you leave out _____?" We had, in fact, a sizable "bench" of additional names we would like to have included—but there were only fifty slots. I confess that in the end, our choices were personal as we sought to hold true to the title criterion of people "every Christian should know."

Let it be noted that none of the fifty was perfect. Each of them harbored human flaws and misassumptions; I have not tried to gloss over these, but to report them charitably. Most of the subjects have over the course of their ministries been on the receiving end of public criticisms—some justified, others unfair. From each case we can learn.

I must give grateful thanks to the following historians, without whose work I could never have developed this book: Frank Bartleman (eyewitness to the Azusa Street awakening), Dr. Vinson Synan, Dr. Mel Robeck, Stanley Frodsham, Dr. Edith Blumhofer, Dr. Stanley Burgess and Dr. Amos Yong. Thank God that these could not only speak in tongues but also write in lucid English.

Having said that, I invite you to give a hearing to this "great cloud of witnesses," men and women who (if I may paraphrase the language of Hebrews 11) by the Spirit preached New Testament truth, healed the sick, cast out dark forces, withstood the arrows of accusation, held true to their calling and even shed light in faraway places—of whom the world was not worthy. Their reward awaits.

1

Maria Woodworth-Etter
(1844–1924)

The Female Forerunner

S he was only eleven years old that summer day when her father collapsed in a field on their Ohio farm with a fatal sunstroke. Maria (pronounced *muh-RYE-uh*) Underwood and her older siblings would now need to drop out of school and go to work, helping their grieving mother keep food on the table.

And things had been going so well the past year, since her hard-drinking father and his wife had begun attending a nearby Disciples of Christ congregation. There young Maria had heard the Gospel for the first time. She was born again at age thirteen, baptized in a creek—and soon thereafter felt she heard the voice of God saying, "Go to the highways and hedges, and gather the lost sheep." That made no sense to her, in that the Disciples did not accept women in the pulpit. She knew of no other females doing this kind of thing; even Catherine Booth, eventual "Mother of the Salvation Army," did not preach her first sermon (across the ocean) until 1860. Women in America could not even vote, for that matter.

The only way forward, she assumed, would be to marry a Christian man along whose side she could work. In her late teens, she married Philo Horace Woodworth, a nearby farmer. Six children came along rapidly—and with them, one heartache upon another, as five succumbed by the age of seven. (She later wrote about their dying moments in agonizing detail.) Only the oldest, a daughter, lived to adulthood.

It was not until she reached the age of 35 that she dared to speak publicly, in a meeting of the Society of Friends (Quakers), which had always welcomed women in ministry. When she got up to speak, she was given a vision of the pit of hell, with unwary people falling into it. She cried out for her audience to be saved from such horror. The response was immediate.

Soon thereafter, she received another riveting vision in the night. Her description:

> The dear Savior stood by me . . . and asked what I was doing on earth. I felt condemned and said, "Lord, I am going to work in thy vineyard."
>
> The Lord said, "When?"
>
> And I answered, "When I get prepared for the work."
>
> Then the Lord said to me, "Don't you know that while you are getting ready, souls are perishing? Go now, and I will be with you."
>
> I told him that I could not talk to the people; I did not know what to say, and they would not listen to me.
>
> Jesus said: "You can tell the people what the Lord has done for your soul; tell of the glory of God and the love of Jesus;

tell sinners to repent and prepare for death and the Judgment, and I will be with you."

Still I made one excuse after another, and Jesus would answer, "Go, and I will be with you."

From that point forward in the 1880s, she began to hold public meetings in her area. People swarmed to hear her, and to respond to her salvation call. Regarding one 1883 meeting in Fairview, Ohio, she wrote:

> I felt impressed that God was going to restore love and harmony in the church. . . . [Those] present came to the altar, made a full consecration, and prayed for a baptism of the Holy Ghost and fire. That night it came. Fifteen came to the altar screaming for mercy. Men and women fell and lay like dead. I felt it was the work of God, but did not know how to explain it or what to say. I was a little frightened. . . .
>
> The ministers and old saints wept and praised the Lord. . . . They said it was the Pentecost power, that the Lord was visiting them in great mercy and power. . . .

Soon she felt God calling her to also pray for the sick. At first she resisted this, fearing it would distract from evangelism. The Lord assured her that if she prayed for the sick, *more* people would come and be saved. She obeyed.

As the meetings became more dramatic, her husband became more skeptical, wishing Maria would remain a quiet farmer's wife. He gradually grew hostile and began drinking heavily as well as seducing some of the women who came to his wife's meetings. There was also evidence of some mental imbalance, perhaps a reaction to the deaths of his five children. By the late 1880s, Philo and Maria had separated, and they were divorced in 1891. He quickly remarried but died of typhoid fever within a year of the divorce; Maria conducted his funeral.

Meanwhile, her travels gradually took her across America, from Chicago to Atlanta to San Francisco to Kansas City. Accounts of healing cures began to pile up: chorea (involuntary jerking of the shoulders, hips and face), spinal meningitis, cancer, deafness, misshapen limbs and shoulders that had never healed correctly following an accident. In 1889 she purchased a tent that could seat eight thousand, setting it up for the first time in Oakland, California. "The power of God was all over the congregation, and around the city," she remembered.

> The Holy Ghost would fall on the people while we were preaching. The multitude would be held still, like as though death was in their midst. Many of the most intelligent and best dressed men would fall back in their seats, with their hands held up to God, being held up under the mighty power of God. Men and women fell, all over the tent, like trees in a storm; some would have visions of God.

More than once, her tent became too small for the crowds. Her largest audience was apparently a camp meeting five miles outside Alexandria, Indiana, with an estimated crowd of 25,000. The people had to listen carefully, since no sound amplification was yet on hand in those days. From a high platform in a grove, "I talked nearly two hours. The people all stood. The solemnity of death rested upon the multitude. Some had their bodies healed, and thousands were brought to Christ."

In view of the manifestations, some newspapers began to dub her the "Trance Evangelist." She compared the falling with what happened to the apostle Peter in Acts 10, when God had to immobilize him before he would agree to take the Gospel to Cornelius and his household.

In Framingham, Massachusetts, she was arrested for practicing medicine without a license, but she was released when too many citizens came forward with credible accounts of their healings. The same thing happened in Fremont, Nebraska (outside Omaha). Her only defense: "The power of God which was given to the apostles in their day has never been taken from the church. Let the Holy Ghost work in any way that agrees with the Word of God."

In St. Louis in 1890, local psychiatrists filed charges of insanity against her for claiming that she saw visions of God. One night, a gang surrounded her tent. The once-timid farm girl wrote:

They had pistols and clubs, and were ready to kill us, and tear down the tent. It looked as if we would all be killed. Several ministers tried to talk, but were stoned down, or their voice drowned out. It looked like surrender or death.

It was an awful sight to see a little band of Christians, sitting nearly frozen to their seats with fear, surrounded by a mob of wild, fierce men and women, many of them half-drunk, their eyes and faces red and inflamed. . . .

I said to my co-workers, "We will never give up, and if they take us out of the tent before we are ready to go, they will take us out dead." I told them to lead in prayer one after the other, and the God of Elijah would answer. . . .

A feeling of the awful Presence of God began to fall on the people. . . . Then I arose, and . . . raised my hand in the name of the Lord and commanded them to listen. I said the Lord had sent me there to do them good, and that I would not leave until the Lord told me to, when our work was done. I told them the

Lord would strike dead the first one that tried to harm us or to strike us with a dagger.

The power of God fell, and the fear of God came upon all the multitude. The sweat came on their faces, and they stood like as though in a trance; the men began to take their pipes out of their mouths, and their hats off. . . . They felt they stood naked and guilty before God. . . . Tears ran down many faces, through the dirt, leaving streaks. . . .

They all passed out quietly. After that, the hoodlum element always respected me.

Her meetings in Los Angeles during the winter of 1893–94 ran on for five weeks. Along the way of her travels, in 1902 she married a man she met in Arkansas, Samuel Etter, who supported her ministry. She added his last name to her own, forming a hyphenated surname—an unusual move in those times.

She watched the 1906 awakening at the Azusa Street Mission from a distance, not sure at first whether its teaching was valid. But soon she came to embrace the Pentecostal message demonstrated there, first speaking in tongues herself in 1912 at the age of 68. That same year saw another nearly five-month run of meetings in Dallas, where she preached three meetings a day. She spoke at the 1913 "Worldwide Camp Meeting" near Pasadena, California, where, according to one published report, "Many were healed as Sister Etter raised her hands toward heaven while she was leaving the tent."

Samuel Etter died the following year. Maria was present in Hot Springs, Arkansas, for the 1914 organizing of the Assemblies of God—although she noticed that some of the men in charge were careful not to give her "too much authority." Nevertheless, Assemblies historian Carl Brumback later honored her by writing, "She looked just like your grandmother, but . . .

exercised tremendous spiritual authority over sin, disease, and demons."

Her books sold widely and were abridged for editions in French, Italian, Danish, Swedish, Egyptian and Hindi, among others. As her strength weakened in her final years, she sometimes had to be carried to the meetings, where she would stand to preach—and then be carried home again. She retired to open a tabernacle in Indianapolis (today called Lakeview Church) but kept preaching right up until her death on September 16, 1924, a praise of tongues upon her lips. She is buried there next to her daughter and son-in-law.

She was, in a sense, a John-the-Baptist type forerunner of the coming Pentecostal and charismatic awakenings—bold, unconventional and controversial at times, but undeniably anointed by God to bring salvation, healing and divine power to the world.

2

Smith Wigglesworth
(1859–1947)

Bold as a Lion

Fifteen-year-old Kenneth Ware was hurrying down the street one day, when suddenly a man's voice rang out: "Come here, boy! Put out your tongue!" He had never seen the man before. And he hadn't even introduced himself.

But Kenneth did not have the nerve to run off. He did what the man ordered. The teenager said not a word, because he knew if he tried, he would only stutter. His speech impediment had been a serious drawback for as long as he could remember.

Before he knew what was happening, the audacious man reached out and grabbed his tongue! "Lad, this tongue will preach the Gospel," he announced. And then he walked away.

From that moment forward, young Kenneth never stuttered again. He preached his first sermon at the age of seventeen and became a lifelong missionary, especially to Jewish refugees in France.

The stranger who had stopped him on the street was none other than the bold British evangelist Smith Wigglesworth, whose spiritual gifts of the word of knowledge, healing and miracles could be downright shocking at times. He, like the boy, had grown up with major limitations—not physically, but in terms of opportunity. He had been put to work in a mill by the age of seven; as a result, he received no formal schooling. He learned to read only in his mid-twenties, when his wife taught him. He managed to support his family (he eventually had five children) by working as a plumber in the northern English town of Bradford.

One thing was sure in his mind, however—that he belonged to Christ as the result of being saved at the age of eight in a Methodist revival meeting. He had been confirmed by an Anglican bishop, baptized by immersion in a Baptist church and instructed about the Bible by a Plymouth Brethren friend. In his late teens, young Smith was drawn to the Salvation Army, where he took up street evangelism. He also met a gifted young woman who could preach well, Polly Featherstone. They married in 1882.

He stayed in her shadow for many years, until he began to hear about "divine healing" and the "baptism in the Holy Spirit." Hungry for a greater spiritual reality, he sought this baptism and finally received it when an Anglican vicar's wife, Mary Boddy, laid hands on him, prayed—and then left the room. But unexpectedly (he said later), "The fire fell. The joy was so great that when I came to utter it my tongue failed, and I began to worship God in other tongues as the Spirit gave me utterance."

Back home, Polly was less than impressed with his exuberant report. "I have been preaching for twenty years," she said, "and you have sat beside me on the platform. But on Sunday you will preach yourself, and I'll see what there is in it." Up to this point, any pulpit attempts by Smith had broken down within two or three minutes, requiring Polly to step up and rescue the service.

The next Sunday was an entirely different story. Smith Wigglesworth held forth confidently from Isaiah 61:1–3: "The Spirit of the Lord GOD is upon me, because the LORD hath anointed me to preach good tidings . . ." (verse 1 KJV). Polly sat slackjawed in the back of the mission, eventually sputtering aloud, "That's not my Smith, Lord; that's not my Smith!"

From that day forward, his ministry grew by leaps and bounds, eventually replacing the plumbing business. People were saved and healed in his meetings. Sometimes results emerged even at a long distance. Once a woman came to him worried about her son's marriage. The young man had served the Lord originally, but now the marriage was in such bad shape that he had moved back in with his mother.

Wigglesworth was not intimidated in the least. "Give me your handkerchief," he said to the woman. He put it between his hands and said, "Lord, smite this young man with conviction!" He then returned the handkerchief to the woman and told her to put it under her son's pillow, saying nothing.

That night, the son did not return home until late. His mother was already in bed. He went to his room, got ready for bed and crawled in. Immediately, he was seized with a terrible feeling. He soon got out of bed, fell on his knees and repented before God. Then he got dressed again, awakened his mother and said, "Don't worry, Mum. I'm going back home. I'll see you tomorrow."

And in fact, the young couple had a wonderful reconciliation.

Wigglesworth's booming voice left little room for debate. His grammar was never perfect (except, curiously, when he would interpret a message in tongues). A man once teased him after receiving one of his letters, "You know, you spelled the title of the Holy Spirit seven different ways in your letter."

The evangelist was not embarrassed. "Did you understand it?" he asked.

"Oh, yes."

"Then thank God," Wigglesworth said. "That's all that matters." He was in some ways like the early apostles, of whom the Bible says, "When they saw the courage of Peter and John and realized that they were unschooled, ordinary men, they were astonished and they took note that these men had been with Jesus" (Acts 4:13).

Polly Wigglesworth passed away in 1913; she was only 51. For the next three decades, her husband traveled more than ever, to the European continent, to America, to Africa and beyond. Two books of his sermons, *Ever-Increasing Faith* and *Faith that Prevails*, were widely welcomed. The theme song of his meetings was usually the simple chorus "Only believe, only believe; all things are possible, only believe."

He had no interest in what medical science might accomplish. He was absolutely fearless in confronting the work of Satan, which is what he considered disease to be. If someone had stomach trouble, for example, he was not beyond hitting the person's abdomen with his fist as he prayed! When questioned about this tactic, he said, "I don't hit people; I hit the Devil. If they get in the way, I can't help it." And once the shock wore off, the sufferers often found they had, in fact, been made whole.

When he went to Sweden for a campaign, the government forbade him to *touch* anyone for whom he prayed. Wigglesworth asked the Lord what to do. He felt led to ask instead for everyone with a physical need to stand, or at least to raise their hand, then lay hands on their own body area in need while he led a prayer for healing from the platform. The power of God swept through the huge audience, with hundreds receiving their miracle.

Wigglesworth's son-in-law, James Salter, who often accompanied him in his travels, said, "We never knew what he was going to do next. We were always afraid he would go 'too far.' But he never did. He always said, 'You can't go too far with God; in fact, you can't go far enough.'"

One time he was staying with a Church of England curate who had suffered the amputation of both legs below the knee. In those days, few prosthetics were available to help such a person.

After dinner, Wigglesworth suddenly blurted out to the man, "Go and get a new pair of shoes in the morning."

What?!! Was this some kind of cruel joke? The minister hardly knew how to take this directive. But during the night, he sensed God saying to him, *Do as My servant hath said.* The man could get no sleep the rest of the night.

Early the next morning, he got into his wheelchair and was waiting downtown when the shoe store opened. He went in and sat down. When the clerk came, he said, "Would you get me a pair of shoes, please?"

"Yes, sir. Size and color?" Then the clerk glanced down at the man's legs and said, "I'm sorry, sir. We can't help you."

"It's all right, young man," the curate replied. "But I do want a pair of shoes. Size eight, color black."

The clerk could not think what else to do but to go get the requested shoes. When he returned with the box, the curate proceeded to put one stump into a shoe—and immediately a foot and leg formed! He moved on to the other stump—and the same thing happened again. He walked out of the shop with not only a new pair of shoes but also a new pair of legs.

When the man got back home, Wigglesworth was not surprised. He had fully expected this to happen. "As far as God is concerned," he claimed, "there is no difference between forming a limb and healing a broken bone."

Those who knew Wigglesworth closely said that over the course of his active ministry, fourteen different people were raised from the dead.

Late in his life, he was ministering in South Africa when a significant prophecy came. One morning about seven o'clock he came barging into the office of his local host, David du Plessis (head of the Apostolic Faith Mission). Laying his hands on the man's shoulders and, in fact, pushing him against the wall, he began to speak on God's behalf:

> You have been in "Jerusalem" long enough. . . . I will send you to the uttermost parts of the earth. . . . You will bring the message of Pentecost to all churches . . . you will travel more than evangelists do. . . . God is going to revive the churches in the last days and through them turn the world upside down. Even the Pentecostal movement will become a mere joke compared with the revival which God will bring through the churches.[1]

To read the remarkable fulfillment of this prophecy given in 1936, see this book's profiles of David du Plessis (chapter 13) and other Episcopalians, Lutherans, and Catholics throughout.

3

Charles H. Mason
(1866–1961)

The Man Who Said, "Yes, Lord"

A few heads might have turned at the Azusa Street Mission when, in March 1907, Charles H. Mason and two associates showed up. Anyone who would have gotten to know them would have learned they had ridden the train nearly two thousand miles, from Memphis, Tennessee, to come see and experience the Spirit's activity.

A few more questions would have revealed that Mason, at the age of 42, was an ordained minister and, in fact, co-founder of a collection of black Holiness or "sanctified" churches across the mid-South called the Church of God in Christ (COGIC). He had come up with that name one day while walking along a street in Little Rock, basing it upon the language of 1 Thessalonians 2:14 and 2 Thessalonians 1:1. The group was already legally registered and ordaining clergy.

Mason himself had been ordained by the Missionary Baptists and had graduated from the Minister's Institute at Arkansas Baptist College. His ongoing spiritual quest led him, however, to seek sanctification as a distinct work of grace, which did not go over well with the Baptist Convention. By the late 1890s, he and a colleague were busy preaching the Holiness message in churches and camp meetings, calling listeners to a deeper walk with God.

Then came news of a revival in Los Angeles. Mason simply had to go see for himself.

> The first day in the meeting I sat to myself, away from those that went with me. I began to thank God in my heart for all things, for when I heard some speak in tongues, I knew it was right though I did not understand it. Nevertheless, it was sweet to me.
>
> I also thank God for Elder [William J.] Seymour, who came and preached a wonderful sermon. His words were sweet and powerful. . . . When he closed his sermon, he said, "All of those that want to be sanctified or baptized with the Holy Ghost, go to the upper room; and all those that want to be justified, come to the altar."
>
> I said that is the place for me. . . . Glory![1]

While Mason was pleased to see the multiracial gathering of believers, all seeking God's abundance, he wasn't entirely comfortable when white brothers sought to pray with him for the Spirit's outpouring. After all, he had lost his sharecropper father as a twelve-year-old boy when a yellow-fever epidemic swept through, and nearby hospitals would not treat blacks. A year later, he himself had been stricken with apparent tuberculosis; only the desperate prayers of his mother and her friends pulled him back to health. Did these whites at Azusa Street truly have his best interests at heart?

"That night," he later recounted, "the Lord spoke to me that Jesus saw all of this world's wrongs but did not attempt to set [them] right until God overshadowed Him with the Holy Ghost. And He said I was no better than my Lord, and if I wanted Him to baptize me, I would have to let . . . rights and wrongs alone and look to Him. So I said yes to God."

Back at the mission . . .

The Spirit came upon the saints and upon me. . . . Then I gave up for the Lord to have His way within me. So there came a wave of Glory into me, and all of my being was filled with the Glory of the Lord.

So when He had gotten me straight on my feet, there came a light which enveloped my whole being above the brightness of the sun. When I opened my mouth to say "Glory," a flame touched my tongue which ran down me. My language changed, and no word could I speak in my own tongue. Oh! I was filled with the Glory of the Lord. My soul was then satisfied.[2]

Charles Mason—the only denominational head to actually visit the mission—stayed in the Azusa Street atmosphere for more than a month before returning to Memphis. There he immediately began to share what the Spirit had done in his life. His friend and COGIC co-founder, Charles Price Jones, was not convinced, however, and after days and nights of intense debate, the two separated. By the fall of 1907, Mason was able to reconstitute COGIC as a clearly Pentecostal body, serving as general overseer and starting a new periodical, *The Whole Truth*.

The next half-dozen years were exciting times of growth, as ministers of both races sought ordination at Mason's hand. There were as many white COGIC churches in that period as black ones. Unfortunately, the prevailing segregation of American culture began to seep into Christian circles, until the call for a general council in April 1914 to form a new association (the Assemblies of God) was sent to whites only. Mason did attend that council in Hot Springs, Arkansas, and was even asked to speak on Thursday night to the four hundred white preachers who had gathered (many of whom held COGIC credentials). But a formal embrace of COGIC was not to be done. The interracial fabric of Azusa Street was unraveling.

Mason was not sidetracked by this. He continued to preach and build up the churches under his care. He commissioned traveling evangelists, established an annual "International Holy Convocation" (which draws large attendance to this day) and set up departments for women's ministry, Sunday school and young people. When he preached, he would often migrate seamlessly from speaking to singing to praying. His signature song was "Yes, yes, yes, yes, yes, yes, yes, Lord." He became known for leading three- to four-hour prayer meetings as well as all-night prayer vigils, called "shut-ins."

When America entered World War I in 1917, Mason (like many other early Pentecostals) took a pacifist stand; he could not abide the drafting of young African American men to advance freedom in Europe while enduring racism and discrimination at home. He called it a "rich man's war and a poor man's fight" and urged his associates to seek conscientious-objector status instead. For this, the FBI opened an investigation of him and even arrested him in Lexington, Mississippi, for allegedly preaching against the war. A white lawyer (and former Nazarene preacher) traveled to Lexington and posted a $2,000 cash bond to get Mason released.

His leadership as presiding bishop continued undeterred, and COGIC continued to grow. His style was "soft-spoken, but firm," according to one historian. By 1945 a huge church complex was dedicated in Memphis, including a 3,700-seat auditorium known today as Mason Temple, where he is buried. Many people do not realize that it was from this pulpit that Martin Luther King Jr. delivered his iconic sermon "I've Been to the Mountaintop" on April 3, 1968—only to be assassinated the next afternoon.

COGIC, meanwhile, has become one of the top-five church bodies in America, with more than six and a half million U.S. communicants, plus one to three million more overseas. The C. H. Mason Seminary is part of Atlanta's International Theological Center. COGIC musicians of note include Walter and Edwin Hawkins ("Oh Happy Day"); Andraé Crouch and his twin sister, Sandra ("My Tribute—To God Be the Glory"); and the Winans family, including BeBe and CeCe.

How fitting that in Los Angeles today—where Charles Mason came with a searching heart long ago—the largest congregation in the city is West Angeles Church of God in Christ, with some 25,000 members; its senior pastor, Charles E. Blake, was elected COGIC presiding bishop in 2007. The effects of one man, ignited by the Holy Spirit, continue to ripple outward for the blessing not only of African American believers, but the entire body of Christ.

4

William J. Seymour
(1870–1922)

Ignition on Azusa Street

D ay after day, he sat alone in the hallway of a small Bible school in Houston, leaning forward to hear as much of the classroom lecture as he could. This son of former slaves would gladly have taken a seat inside with the white students, but the Jim Crow laws of that era would not allow it.

What most filled the mind of William Seymour, this single, short, stocky, 35-year-old evangelist, was not the racial bias but instead what he was learning about the baptism in the Holy Spirit. He was certainly familiar with the concept—it being widely proclaimed throughout the nineteenth century by Holiness and "Deeper Life" preachers, even the notable Charles G. Finney, Dwight L. Moody, and A. J. Gordon. But here, the instructor was attaching something outward and audible to the experience: speaking in tongues. Seymour listened to the teacher's various Scriptures and came to nod his head in agreement.

Not long after, a fellow student passed his name along to a small Holiness church in Los Angeles in search of a pastor. Seymour made his way west, and in February 1906 stood to give his inaugural sermon. He boldly chose as his text Acts 2:4 (KJV, of course): "And they were all filled with the Holy Ghost, and began to speak with other tongues, as the Spirit gave them utterance"—even though he had not yet spoken in tongues himself.

The reception was not encouraging; when Seymour returned for the Sunday evening service, he found the building tightly locked. A couple named Edward and Mattie Lee gave him temporary lodging, and those who had accepted his message began to hold prayer meetings in the humble four-room home of Richard and Ruth Asberry at 214 N. Bonnie Brae Street. On April 9, just as Seymour was about to leave for the prayer meeting, Edward Lee asked for prayer in order to receive the baptism he had heard Seymour speak about. Seymour obliged him, and Lee suddenly began to give glory to God in tongues.

At the meeting that night, the surprised Seymour told what had happened. A time of earnest prayer broke out; by the end of the evening, seven people were praising God in languages they had never studied. One young woman, a maid who worked at a home across the street, went to the piano and began to play beautifully, having had no music lessons in her life. Her gift proved to be permanent.

The news spread rapidly throughout the city, with crowds growing by the hour. The meetings ran around the clock for the next three days. Seymour was forced to preach from the front porch, which eventually collapsed under the weight of the people. A new site would have to be found.

And that is how the Azusa Street Mission began on April 15, in an abandoned church building on a side street less than a mile north of downtown LA, next to a lumberyard, a tombstone shop and some stables. Seating in the ground-level room was no more than rough planks nailed to empty barrels; the upstairs had a prayer room and several sleeping rooms, where Seymour and several associates came to reside.

The daily meetings began at 10 a.m. and continued throughout the rest of the day and late into the evening. As many as a thousand people came on a given day—or tried to listen through the windows. Frank Bartleman, a journalist who reported for various Christian publications, wrote,

> There was no pride there. The service ran almost continuously. Seeking souls could be found under the power almost any hour, day or night. People came to meet God. . . . In that old building, with its low rafters and bare floor, God took strong men and women to pieces, and put them together again for His glory. It was a tremendous overhauling process. Pride, self-assertion, self-importance, and self-esteem could not survive there.
>
> No subjects or sermons were announced ahead of time and no special speakers for such an hour. No one knew what might be coming, what God would do. All was spontaneous, all of the Spirit. We wanted to hear from God through whomever He might speak. We had no "respect of persons". . . .
>
> When we first reached the meeting we avoided as much as possible human contact and greeting. We wanted to meet God first. We got our head under some bench in the corner in prayer and met [others] only in the Spirit. . . . The meetings started themselves, spontaneously, in testimony, praise, and worship.[1]

As a result, literally hundreds were saved. Hundreds experienced physical healings. Verbal expressions from the Spirit were welcomed. Among the songs that frequently rang out was "The Comforter has come, the Comforter has come—the Holy Ghost from heav'n, the Father's promise giv'n. . . ."

On April 18, the *Los Angeles Times* ran a scorching front-page story, with headlines that read:

Weird Babble of Tongues
New Sect of Fanatics Is Breaking Loose
Wild Scene Last Night on Azusa Street
Gurgle of Wordless Talk by a Sister

It said that "the night is made hideous in the neighborhood by the howlings of the worshippers, who spend hours swaying forth and back in a nerve-wracking attitude of prayer and supplication." Seymour himself was mocked as "an old colored exhorter" (he was only 35) who hypnotized people with his "stony optic" (a glass replacement for his right eye, which had failed during an earlier siege of smallpox).

On the other hand, a minister named Arthur Osterberg, who had helped lead the cleanup of the building, described Seymour as "meek and plain spoken and no orator. He spoke the common language of the uneducated class. He might preach for three-quarters of an hour with no more emotion than that there post. He was no arm-waving thunderer, by any stretch of the imagination."

There was no pulpit—only two crates stacked vertically, into which Seymour sometimes tucked his head for long stretches of prayer during the meetings. There was no choir; in fact, no musical instruments. No offerings were collected; only a small box on the wall carried the sign SETTLE WITH THE LORD.

The open flow of worship and exhortation was hard to manage sometimes because not all were pure-hearted in their desire to participate. Seymour had to give stern corrections from time to time. One day he commented, "I need to say something important. We got too many folk comin' in here a-seeking the tongues. When you go down to the shoe store, you don't say to the clerk, 'I want to buy a pair o' tongues.' You just buy the shoes—and the tongues come with 'em.

"Folks need to just be seekin' the Holy Ghost. The tongues part will take care of itself."

In addition to the unstructured meetings, visitors were equally surprised, in this highly segregated era, by the multiracial makeup of the Azusa crowd. Whites, blacks, Mexicans, Chinese and other ethnicities sat (or stood, or knelt) shoulder to shoulder in the meetings. An iconic photo of the leadership team shows three blacks and eight Caucasians. (Five are men; six are women.) In the oft-quoted line from Frank Bartleman, "The color line was washed away in the Blood." Seymour, in fact, heralded the racial harmony of the awakening as an equal sign, along with tongues, of the Spirit's invasion.

Visitors from other parts of the United States (indeed, the world) had to swallow hard at first. When G. B. Cashwell, a North Carolina evangelist, came to see what was happening, his Southern traditions were quite offended. "Chills went down my spine," he later admitted, when a young black man walked over and placed his hands on Cashwell's head. But after a few services, "I lost my pride," he said, asking Seymour and several other blacks to lay hands on him in order to receive the Pentecostal experience. He returned home to begin spreading the message far and wide.

The same dynamic, in reverse, played out when blacks found themselves at close range with white brothers and sisters.

As the daily meetings continued for the next three and a half years, the Azusa fire spread far and wide, to Canada, Europe,

India, Australia and various African nations. Christian critics made their views known, of course. G. Campbell Morgan, renowned Congregationalist pastor of Westminster Chapel (London) and popular preacher across America as well, castigated the goings-on at Azusa Street as "the last vomit of Satan." Phineas F. Bresee in nearby Pasadena, first general superintendent of what was then called the Pentecostal Church of the Nazarene, took steps eventually to shorten the group's name by dropping its first word. Even Seymour's onetime mentor from the Houston Bible school, Charles F. Parham, was dismayed when he came to visit Azusa and saw all the "race-mixing."

Seymour did not attempt to refute those who found the Azusa Street revival too eccentric, too extreme or too emotional. He simply set forth his guiding principle (in an *Apostolic Faith* newspaper article, September 1907), as follows:

> We are measuring everything by the Word, every experience must measure up with the Bible. Some say that is going too far [i.e., being too restrictive], but if we have lived too close to the Word, we will settle that with the Lord when we meet Him in the air.

The eminent theologian and social critic Harvey Cox (Harvard Divinity School) said it well in his insightful book *Fire from Heaven* when he observed:

> Like the story of the ancient Israelites and the life of Jesus of Nazareth, [the modern Pentecostal Movement] is another example of the way God uses unlikely vessels . . . to accomplish the divine purpose. Pouring the new blessing on a one-eyed black preacher and a gaggle of social outcasts is like choosing a nation of slaves and the son of an unwed mother to begin new chapters of history.[2]

5

John G. Lake
(1870–1935)

Make Room for the Healer

He certainly did not set out in life to become a missionary with a healing ministry. In fact, his growing-up years in his native Canada were beset by one family illness after another. "Our church had diligently taught us that the days of miracles were past," he wrote many years later. "Believing thus, eight members of the family had been permitted to die."

But new light came flooding into John G. Lake's heart when first his brother, then two sisters and finally his wife, Jennie, were all dramatically pulled back from major afflictions (kidney failure, breast cancer, nonstop hemorrhaging and tuberculosis) through the message and prayers at Zion City, Illinois, founded by the controversial John Alexander Dowie. Over the next eight years, "every answer to prayer, every miraculous touch of God, every response of my own soul to the Spirit had created within me a more intense longing for an intimacy and a consciousness of God, like I felt the disciples of Jesus and the primitive church had possessed."

In late 1907, Lake left his business career in the insurance field to preach full-time. What financial assets he had built up were given away "in a manner I believed to be in the best interests of the Kingdom of God. . . . [I] made myself wholly dependent upon God for the support of myself and my family. . . . I preached every day to large congregations, saw a multitude of people saved from their sins and healed of their diseases, and hundreds of them baptized in the Holy Ghost."

As if this was not radical enough, he soon felt the Lord tell him distinctly, *In the spring, you will go to Africa.* How would this be possible, now that he no longer had any savings? He and his preaching colleague, Thomas Hezmalhalch, began to pray—and mysteriously, an envelope with four $500 checks showed up in the mail. They bought tickets and set sail the next April as a group: the Lakes with their seven children, Mr. and Mrs. Hezmalhalch, and two other workers.

"We were faith missionaries," John G. Lake recalled. "We had neither a board nor friends behind us to furnish money. We were dependent on God. Many times during that trip to Johannesburg we bowed our heads and reminded God that when we arrived there, we should need a home."

As they got off the train, a small woman came rushing up. "You are an American missionary party?" she asked.

"Yes."

"How many are there in your family?"

Lake replied, "My wife, myself and seven children."

"Oh, you are the family!" the woman instantly answered. "The Lord has sent me to meet you, and I want to give you a home." Within hours they were settled in a furnished cottage.

The two men soon began to preach in a rented hall in the suburb of Doornfontein. Immediately people began to be affected. One night,

> a man of desperately bad character, a spiritualist, came under conviction of sin and found his way into the hall. Soon he heard an audible voice telling him, "Go and ask Lake to pray for you." . . . Lake and Hezmalhalch placed their hands on him, and in a minute he was saved, filled with the Holy Spirit, and praising God in new tongues.
>
> Among others who had entered the hall was the governess [family tutor] of Johannesburg's chief Jewish rabbi, and she was amazed to hear this ex-spiritualist extolling the Lord in pure Hebrew.[1]

But that was not the end of the story. The report continues:

> His brother, a [railroad] stationmaster, was believed to be a man of irreproachable character; and he too became hungry. However, though he prayed and pleaded with God for blessing, nothing happened. He became desperate. . . .
>
> At last in a meeting which lasted until four in the morning, the stationmaster withdrew from his pockets a watch and [a] handful of money, placing these on one side, and within a few minutes he was filled with the Holy Spirit. Those present recognized the German language. Afterwards it transpired that the money he had set aside was some of which he had taken from [blacks], by charging them more than was just for their tickets, while the watch had fallen out of somebody's suitcase; and instead of returning it, he had kept it.
>
> Since the stolen property could not be returned to its owners, it was handed to the evangelists for their work.[2]

43

This fresh provision of funds, however, was the exception rather than the rule. The crowds that came to receive ministry generally assumed that the Americans had a supporting mission society back home, which was not true. More than once, the Lake family went without meals. The power of God in the public meetings was amazing, but in the shadows, desperation grew.

Three days before Christmas that year, Jennie Lake tragically succumbed while still in her late thirties, apparently exhausted and malnourished. Her husband was devastated. Should he quit and go back to America?

He prayed for guidance, and when his sister Irene came to help care for the children, he was able to gradually resume his preaching. Multiple thousands of South Africans—from all races—were forever changed. Miners, farm workers, city folk and youth filled the meetings. So many churches were started that a new collective was set up, the Apostolic Faith Mission of South Africa, which today is the nation's fifth-largest religious body.

In early 1913, after just five years in the South African field, the 43-year-old Lake turned leadership over to a young black preacher named Elias Letwaba, who had once been scorned by a white congregation when Lake had introduced him. Lake had put his arm around the black man's neck and kissed him, calling him "my brother"—which brought hisses and boos from the crowd. Lake turned suddenly to scold them: "My friends, God has made of one blood all nations of men! If you don't want to acknowledge them as your brothers, then you'll have the mortification of going away into eternal woe, while you see many of these black folk going to eternal bliss."

The crowd persisted in their shouting. "Put out the black devils! Kick them into the street."

Lake, with his hand still on Letwaba's shoulder, replied, "If you turn out these men, then you must turn me out, too, for I will stand by my black brethren."

After bringing his family back to the United States, he traveled to various cities to preach. He took time in November to give his children a loving stepmother by marrying Florence Switzer. "Men in these days consider themselves to be happily married once," he commented. "I have been especially blessed in that I have been happily married twice."

By the following July, the couple settled in Spokane, Washington, where Lake pastored a church and began to open what he called "divine healing rooms"—quiet places where teams of believers would take weekday appointments with the sick, read Scripture to them and then lay hands on them for recovery. Records were kept, documenting that ten thousand people experienced healing in the first sixteen months the rooms were open. The city was so stirred that the Better Business Bureau appointed a committee to investigate the many stories appearing in local newspapers.

When Lake stood before the committee, he brought along eighteen individuals to tell how they had been healed. He then presented the committee with the names of many others they could interview for themselves. Furthermore, he invited them to a public meeting in the large Masonic Temple on Sunday, June 23, where one hundred different cases would be showcased.

The committee started interviewing, and by Friday, June 21, they sent Lake a letter saying the Sunday meeting would not be necessary after all. Two members came to see Lake privately, saying, "We soon found out upon investigation, you did not tell half of it."

Lake went ahead with the Sunday meeting anyway before a standing-room-only crowd. Testimony after testimony went on throughout the afternoon, affirming freedom from seizures, cancer, a gallstone operation gone wrong, a fibroid tumor, paralysis and a baby's congenital malformation of the skull. When Lake said, "All persons who have been healed by the power of God and who desire to add their testimony to those who have already been given, stand," 276 people rose up. The meeting then closed with prayer.

In 1920 the Lakes moved from Spokane to Portland, Oregon, where history repeated itself. Gordon Lindsay (eventual publisher of the *Voice of Healing* magazine in the 1950s and beyond; see chapter 14) remembers going to the Portland church as a boy and seeing "a certain corner reserved for . . . crutches, casts, and various other paraphernalia which had been discarded by people who once had serious disabilities. It became evident to us that God's power was mightily in evidence in this assembly, or else there was being perpetrated one of the greatest hoaxes the city of Portland had ever witnessed."

If you search the Internet today, you can find a skeptic or two who asserts that John G. Lake was a source of tall tales; Barry Morton, a research fellow at Indiana University, published a 2012 journal piece calling Lake "a fraud, con man and false prophet" for lack of independent verification. His accusation, however, was rebutted in 2016 in another journal by Dr. Marius Nel of North-West University (in South Africa) for his "seemingly preconceived notion of Lake . . . supported by an unbalanced utilization and unfair treatment of sources."[3]

Lake invested his sunset years in opening more "healing rooms" up and down the West Coast (a format that continues to this day nearly a century later, based either inside church buildings or in commercial spaces that look and function very much like medical clinics). At his memorial service, the speaker said, "He has left his mark indelibly upon the world of gospel truth. . . . He found us in sickness. He found us in poverty of spirit. He found us in despair, but he revealed to us such a Christ as we had never dreamed of knowing this side of heaven. We thought victory was over there, but Dr. Lake revealed to us that victory was here, a present and possible reality. . . . A light shone in the darkness and we, who found Christ at last as He really is, only had words as the words of Thomas who said, 'My Lord and my God.'"[4]

6

F. F. Bosworth
(1877–1958)

Listening for the Voice

The evangelist was nervous. The local pastor, who had invited him to Lima, Ohio, had specifically asked him to preach on divine healing. F. F. Bosworth certainly believed God could heal the sick; in fact, he himself had been rescued from tuberculosis as a teenager when a Methodist "Bible woman" had prayed for him. Then in 1912, as the founding pastor of a Christian and Missionary Alliance church in Dallas, he had seen the dramatic results of Maria Woodworth-Etter's five-month tent meeting (see chapter 1).

But while numerous people were now getting saved in Bosworth's evangelistic meetings, he had not yet ventured to give a healing message of his own. In prayer, he asked, "Lord, suppose I preach on healing, and the people come and don't get healed?"

The voice of God seemed to respond, *If people didn't get saved, you wouldn't stop preaching the Gospel.*

From that moment on—and for the next four decades—the man proclaimed on the basis of Exodus 15:26, Psalm 103:3, Isaiah 53:5, and other Scriptures that healing was as central to the Good News as salvation was. And afflicted people were made whole by the tens of thousands.

Among them were more than a few of the deaf. In Chicago, where he eventually headquartered, the *Chicago Daily News* reported that as a result of his visit to a school for the deaf, so many students were miraculously healed that the school ending up shutting its doors. At a January 1921 meeting in Detroit, a woman was healed of blindness. In Pittsburgh, a well-known veteran of World War I who had suffered a mustard gas attack in France and, after fourteen surgeries, had lost his voice was prayed for. Instantly he began shouting, "Praise the Lord! Praise the Lord!"—then looked for a telephone to call his mother with the good news. The next day's newspaper headline read, "John Sproul Can Talk!"

By 1924, Bosworth's sermons had been compiled into a book entitled *Christ the Healer,* which remains a classic to this day. Among its stirring lines:

> Don't doubt your faith; doubt your doubts, for they are unreliable.
>
> When your eyes are upon your symptoms and your mind is occupied with them more than with God's Word, you have [planted] in the ground the wrong kind of seed for the harvest that you desire. You have in the ground seeds of doubt. You are trying to raise one kind of crop from another kind of seed. It is impossible to sow tares and reap wheat. Your symptoms may point you to death, but God's Word points you to life.[1]

Late in his life, he accepted the challenge of a debate on divine healing with a prominent Baptist minister in Houston named W. E. Best. There, before a large audience, he presented what he saw as the truth about God's healing promises, while Best argued that such things were for the apostolic age only. Eventually Bosworth asked everyone who had been cured by faith to stand. Hundreds arose. After they sat down again, he followed up with "How many of you are Baptists?" According to one newspaper report, "At least 100 stood up."

Yet Bosworth was not pugnacious. Unlike other boisterous Pentecostal evangelists of the day, his speaking style was steady and calm. One Pittsburgh reporter wrote about his meetings, which had been moved to the Carnegie Music Hall after all churches had proved too small, "The simplicity of the services and the wanton lack of any attempt to play upon the emotions of the great throngs who crowd themselves into the building naturally incites the onlooker to inquire, 'What manner of man is this?'" (alluding to Luke 8:25).

He was also noteworthy in that he picked no fights with medical science. In *Christ the Healer,* he wrote:

> I truly thank God for all the help that has ever come to sufferers through the physician, through the surgeon, the hospital and the trained nurse; but, if sickness is the will of God, then, to quote one writer, "Every physician is a lawbreaker; every trained nurse is defying the Almighty; every hospital is a house of rebellion, instead of a house of mercy."[2]

His gracious temperament showed in the matter of whether speaking in tongues was the *only* "initial evidence" of the baptism in the Holy Spirit. Bosworth spoke in tongues himself (following the 1906 laying on of hands by Pentecostal pioneer

Charles Parham), and so did many in his meetings. He was one of the founding fathers of the Assemblies of God, which established tongues as part of "our distinctive testimony." Bosworth saw value in tongues but cited other manifestations of the Spirit's work as well, and when he could not convince his Assemblies brethren of his view, he quietly surrendered his credentials in 1918. He wrote a booklet to lay out his position, *Do All Speak with Tongues?*

He was willing to pay a personal price for matters of conviction. The greatest example is what happened to him back in 1909, while he was still a pastor in Dallas. He had been invited to travel 150 miles south to the town of Hearne, Texas, where a camp meeting of blacks was underway. He, though white, gladly went; after all, his earlier visit to the Azusa Street Mission had shown him that the Holy Spirit had no interest in discriminating by race or gender.

Music filled the air that night, and a number of whites stood around the edges of the tent to listen to Bosworth's message on the love of Christ for all. At the end of the meeting, a gracious white minister came up to invite him to his home to stay overnight. As they walked away, however, a mob of angry white men stormed up from behind with clubs and sticks. They spit and yelled at Bosworth for coming to preach to a black gathering. They ordered him to get out of town.

Bosworth said he would do so and began walking rapidly toward the train station. But before the next train could arrive, the mob attacked him on the platform. "You'll not leave here alive!" they shouted. Knocking him to the ground, they beat him on the back with boat oars and used a baseball bat to break his left wrist. Again, they insisted he must vanish immediately.

The preacher said nothing more. Despite his bleeding and pain, he used his right arm to pick up his suitcase, and he began walking north in the dark. At one point, he tried to flag down a coming train, but failed. It took him two days to get all the way home, where he collapsed in front of his frightened wife. He spent the next month in bed recovering. He later said the ordeal reminded him of the apostles of old, who had rejoiced for being counted worthy to suffer for the name of Jesus.

It must be admitted that his theological compass wasn't perfect. In the mid-1930s, he began to espouse an error called British-Israelism, the notion that the people of the British Isles (and their American cousins) were the direct descendants of the "Ten Lost Tribes" of Israel, and therefore preferred by God. By 1944, however, Bosworth publicly apologized for mistakenly espousing this belief and was welcomed back into fellowship with those who had withdrawn from him.

With the rise of the post–World War II healing evangelists, the elderly Bosworth became something of a mentor. One story illustrates this point: He was invited to preach at a small church pastored by the young T. L. Osborn (who would go on to hold massive crusades in the 1950s, especially in Africa). When Bosworth arrived at the parsonage, Osborn was not available; he was upstairs praying fervently.

"Daddy" Bosworth, as he had come to be known in his later years, sat patiently, listening to the loud and impassioned pleas for God to bless and meet all kinds of needs. When Osborn finally came downstairs, his white-haired guest said, "You know, Tommy, the Lord's an awfully good gentleman. He won't ever butt in as long as you're doing all the talking!"

Such was a man who wanted to hear from God equally as much as to speak for God and be the conduit of His healing power.

7

Francisco Olazábal
(1886–1937)

El Azteca

I t's more than fifteen hundred miles through mountain ranges and across deserts from the Mexican state of Sinaloa to San Francisco, California—and young Francisco was only sixteen years old when he set out to make the trek alone. There, he would stay with relatives and hopefully join a ship's crew to sail the world.

His father had given him no encouragement; in fact, he had abandoned the family after Francisco's mother had left the traditional church to become a fervent *evangélica*. Their son was now on his own in a strange land.

Soon, however, the boy met a successful businessman named George Montgomery, whose various ventures included operating mines back in Mexico. His wife, Carrie Judd Montgomery, was a notable author and minister of healing, and the couple led young Francisco to focus his life and future plans on Christ. They taught him basic Christian doctrines. In order to learn more, he returned to Mexico at the age of 22 for three years of training at the Wesleyan School of Theology in San Luís Potosí. His first Methodist pastorate was a Spanish-speaking congregation in El Paso, Texas. A Methodist bishop ordained him in 1916.

About this time, however, he reconnected with the Montgomerys, who startled him with the news that they were now Pentecostals and spoke in tongues. He attended a prayer meeting in their home, where he was baptized in the Spirit himself. He soon began to preach the fullness of the Spirit's work to all who would listen. A host sponsor in Los Angeles reported, "God has used Olazábal's faithful message to bring the light of Pentecost to many, especially to those who had known him here before in the Methodist Episcopal Church when he used to criticize and persecute 'this way.'"

His ministry kept widening on both sides of the border. At LA's four-thousand-seat Church of the Open Door, Reuben A. Torrey (a protégé of D. L. Moody) invited him to evangelize Spanish speakers across Los Angeles. He pioneered new churches farther north in California as well as across Texas. He became known in Mexico as *El Azteca* ("the Aztec") for his distinctive facial features. Large crowds came to his meetings; here is one of his accounts:

> It was odd the way it started. While [I was] resting in Mexico City, a native minister came to me. He said he had a church large enough to hold four thousand people, and he had a lot of empty pews. He said he could get together fifteen hundred people if I'd come and preach. I couldn't turn him away; who could?

We had fifteen hundred the first night. I preached Christ to them, Christ the Healer and Christ the Savior. They were hungry for it! Two hundred of them came to the altar that night. They just wouldn't listen to me when I told them I wasn't coming back the next night. They said they'd fill the place if I stayed a week.

I didn't believe that, for you know it's against the law [at that point in time] to advertise a religious meeting in Mexico. You can't put up posters or throw out circulars or put notices in the papers; all you can do is to pass it on by word of mouth. That's all they did; by the end of that week, they had forty-five hundred jammed into that church every night. Today, those same people have the largest church in Mexico!

I knew then what I had to do. I spoke in their own tongue, had their own blood in my veins; now I had to cut myself loose . . . and free-lance for the Lord. I had to go after the masses.[1]

Throughout the 1920s and 1930s, Olazábal's revival campaigns took him as far as New York City and Puerto Rico; he also founded a Bible college in Texas as well as some eighty churches in that state alone. His campaign in Spanish Harlem drew more than one hundred thousand people, with the meetings eventually being held in Brooklyn's Calvary Baptist Church.

For a season, he affiliated with the Assemblies of God; then he led a group of Hispanic pastors to form the Latin American Council of Christian Churches—the first such independent body in the United States. This drew the attention of Foursquare founder Aimee Semple McPherson, who coaxed Olazábal and his group to merge with her denomination, but they declined.

In 1937, he was planning to spread his calling even farther through evangelistic campaigns into South America when tragedy struck. A devastating car crash in south Texas inflicted major damage with internal bleeding; he died in a hospital eight days later at the age of 51. Some fifty thousand people attended memorial services in several cities to honor him. His body was returned for burial at Evergreen Cemetery in East Los Angeles.

We will never know how much more Kingdom work Francisco Olazábal could have accomplished in the decades to come. But never after his death could it be claimed that divine healing and Spirit empowerment were simply *gringo* inventions. The boy from Mexico had blossomed into an apostolic leader in whose footsteps many others would follow.

8

Aimee Semple McPherson

(1890–1944)

Everybody's "Sister"

I f you had been a newspaper reader throughout the 1920s and 1930s, hardly a month would have passed without another story about the dramatic, eye-catching, high-energy evangelist Aimee Semple McPherson . . . a farmer's daughter from Ontario, Canada . . . her conversion to Christ as a teenager during a storefront revival led by a Pentecostal preacher named Robert Semple, whom she married less than a year later . . . their preaching tour across the northern United States and Canada . . . their passion to become missionaries in China . . . his tragic death from malaria shortly after landing in Hong Kong, leaving Aimee a widow not quite twenty years old—and eight months' pregnant.

You would have been fascinated to keep reading about her resettling in New York City, where her mother came to help her with her infant daughter . . . Aimee's volunteering with the Salvation Army . . . her acquaintance with Harold McPherson, and their wedding in 1911 . . . the birth of their son, Rolf . . . Harold's work in his wife's shadow, facilitating her ever-growing tent meetings (an uneasy role that eventually ended in their amicable divorce in 1921) . . . her rising profile across the nation, eventually centering in Los Angeles, where she designed and funded the amazing triple-deck 5,300-seat Angelus Temple (the nation's largest church building at the time), filling it as often as three times a day.

You would have been puzzled by her mysterious disappearance in 1926 while she and her secretary swam off Venice Beach—had she drowned? Was she even still alive? Had she run off with her former radio engineer Kenneth Ormiston, who vanished at the same time? She resurfaced five weeks later on the Arizona/Sonora (Mexico) border in terrible shape, saying she had escaped a brutal kidnapping for ransom. But you would have also noted her continued preaching and initiating new outreaches for another eighteen years . . . the tropical fever that weakened her in 1943, and her last crusade in Oakland, California, the next year, where in her hotel room one morning her son found her unresponsive from an apparent accidental overdose of prescription sleeping pills.

But to assess her place in the gallery of Pentecostal leaders, one must get beyond her personal narrative and take note of her remarkable accomplishments for God's Kingdom. Here is an overview:

- She framed what she called the Foursquare Gospel—
  "Jesus our Savior, Baptizer with the Holy Spirit, Healer

and Soon-Coming King," using the New Jerusalem description of Revelation 21:16 (KJV) . . . and no doubt borrowing/adjusting the "Fourfold Gospel" advocated earlier by A. B. Simpson, founder of the Christian and Missionary Alliance ("Jesus our Savior, Sanctifier, Healer and Coming King").

- She was the first woman to preach a sermon on the radio (1922), as well as the first woman to get an FCC license for a full AM radio station (KFSG, "Kall Four Square Gospel") two years later—tangling at one point with the restrictive regulations of Secretary of Commerce Herbert Hoover, future U.S. president. Thanks to uncluttered airwaves, some claimed they picked up her signal on clear nights as far away as Australia.

- When she preached at Angelus Temple, long lines formed hours in advance down Glendale Boulevard with those hoping to get a seat (not all were successful). The rich and famous of Los Angeles sat beside the poor. The power of her messages brought dramatic responses. "Hundreds rushed to the altar in ever-recurrent waves," she wrote, "crying, 'God be merciful.' . . . No less than three altar calls marked some of the services, especially the divine healing services. . . . Moreover hundreds of people at a time were sometimes slain under the power of God, many receiving the baptism of the Holy Ghost."[1] Among those who walked the aisle for salvation was a boy from nearby Orange County named Richard M. Nixon.

- But she didn't only preach. She created elaborate dramas with biblical themes, typing the scripts herself and then staging them with spectacular effects; among her works were gospel adaptations of "The Lone Ranger," "The Trojan Horse" and "The Wizard of Oz." A trumpet player in the pit orchestra at one point was the future Academy Award–winning actor Anthony Quinn. Even Charlie Chaplin was said to have sneaked into a back row to watch the show. Sometimes her productions were staged instead at LA's even larger Shrine Auditorium, which seated 6,300.

- The temple took its dramatic flair outdoors each New Year's Day, entering colorful floats in the Rose Parade. One of them won the Grand Prize in 1925.

- To prepare more evangelists, pastors and missionaries, she launched the Lighthouse for International Foursquare Evangelism (L.I.F.E.) Bible College next door to the church; today it continues as Life Pacific University in suburban San Dimas.

- Her publishing was brisk, starting with a monthly magazine (*The Bridal Call*) even before the Los Angeles era, and continuing over the years with McPherson's books, tracts, hymnals (including more than sixty of her songs), sacred operas and sheet music for soloists and choirs.

- The Angelus Temple Commissary, which opened to serve the poor in 1927, was ever more needful as the Great Depression bore down. Major quantities of food, blankets and clothing were handed out to those in distress.

- She eventually began making ministry trips outside the United States, including a 'round-the-world tour in 1936. She came home deeply troubled about what such figures as Hitler, Mussolini and Stalin were up to, and said so publicly. When World War II broke out, she openly urged her followers to buy War Bonds and help the cause of freedom.

- By the time of her death in 1944, the International Church of the Foursquare Gospel numbered 410 churches with about 29,000 members. Today there are ten times as many members in the United States alone, not to mention millions more in 145 other nations. Angelus Temple continues to be a spiritual lighthouse today in the Echo Park section of Los Angeles and beyond, especially through its Dream Center outreach.

What explains the phenomenon of "Sister Aimee," as the crowds called her? Was it her megawatt personality? Her gutsy boldness to attempt what other women in that era would never have tried? Her media savvy? Her boundless energy? Her rousing oratory?

She would have brushed aside all of these, pointing instead to what she identified in a sermon published in her book *This Is That* as a "real baptism of the Holy Ghost and fire." Her vivid analogy:

Just as the electric light bulb in the finest chandelier in the White House, despite the splendor of its setting, must be connected without a break to the distant powerhouse if it is to give light—so the pastor and the church of Jesus Christ, though they be in the finest cathedral in the land, must have an unobstructed line and a solid connection with the powerhouse of the Holy Spirit if they are to shine and draw perishing multitudes from the darkness of unbelief and worldliness of today.[2]

Her closing prayer in that message:

> Strip us, Lord, of everything, of the world and self and sin. Empty, cleanse, purify these cold hearts of ours. Melt us in humble contrition at Thine own crucified feet. . . .
>
> Baptize us with Your power, endue us with Your might. Give us, Master, nothing short of the mighty power of Acts 2:4, not for our own sake, but for Your name's sake—that as a flaming torch we may be held within Your hand to point the way to others, to lead the lost to Calvary, the Christian to the upper room and the Spirit-filled believer to the harvest fields to glean and work for You.
>
> Then we will see the sinners saved, the sick made whole, believers filled with Your power; then will our altars overflow, our churches be too small. The world is starving for the gospel of power that will meet the crying need of body, soul and spirit.[3]

9

J. E. Stiles
(1890–1959)

The Boat Rocker

The question for J. E. (Jack) Stiles was never whether the Bible taught a genuine, distinct, point-in-time infilling of the Holy Spirit. It was rather *how* to guide Christians into that dimension. And for his approach, he stirred up more than a little dust.

But then, he had always been something of an innovator, an agent for change, one who didn't mind venturing outside the box. Following his graduation from the University of California (Berkeley) in 1916 with a bachelor's degree in agriculture, he went to work for the extension department, teaching farmers up and down the state's fertile Central Valley how to get bigger fruit and vegetable harvests. He taught so many people about building silos to store their crops that they gave him the nickname "Silo Jack."

In the evenings, he would often hold evangelistic meetings for the same folk he'd been instructing all day in the sun. He stayed on their social level; sometimes he even preached in overalls. He wasn't a bombastic pulpit-pounder; he conveyed the Good News about Jesus in a steady voice. After marrying, he took a job with a large nursery company, where he ran a farm in Porterville that grew seedlings for California orchards. If he saved up enough money here, he thought to himself, maybe he could afford to become a pastor in some poor area that couldn't pay him.

Then came the Great Depression. The company went bankrupt, and Stiles had no job. With nothing else to do, he decided he might as well take the ministry plunge right away. Throughout the 1930s, he led Bethel Full Gospel Church in Hayward, California, part of one of the Pentecostal denominations. Ever the visionary, he built a chapel-on-wheels to be pulled behind a car or truck throughout the county so his youth group could hold services for those who couldn't get to town. It had a pulpit, a small organ, and pews for up to forty people—plus even a generator to power the lights.

The prevailing assumption in those days was that the baptism in the Holy Spirit involved an often-lengthy ordeal of "tarrying"—praying and pleading at the church altar for hours on end. (The name came from Jesus' words in the King James rendition of Luke 24:49: "Behold, I send the promise of my Father upon you: but tarry ye in the city of Jerusalem, until ye be endued with power from on high.") Sincere saints sometimes spent years in this quest without realizing their hope and breaking through to speak in tongues like the Acts believers did. The usual explanation was that maybe they weren't spiritual enough, or maybe there was some hidden sin in their lives that needed to be confessed.

Of course, when some new person with a checkered past showed up at church, got saved and soon received the Holy Spirit in an outpouring of tongues, the old-timers couldn't help thinking, *Wait a minute—this isn't fair!*

Jack Stiles began searching the Scriptures more diligently about all this. He paid special attention to how often he read about the *gift* of the Holy Spirit (Acts 2:38; 8:20; 10:45; 11:17). You don't groan and struggle and cry in order to receive a *gift,* do you? His understanding was stretched when British Bible school leader Howard Carter came to hold meetings in Oakland. There, Stiles watched as people quickly received the Holy Spirit in response to the laying on of hands. Carter spent time talking with Stiles and even invited him to help in the services. This opened the floodgates; within weeks back in the Hayward church, some 22 members had been filled with the Spirit as their pastor gave them simple instruction and then laid hands on them.

Stiles realized this approach was not really new; it followed what had happened in the Samaria revival (Acts 8), the ministry of the layman Ananias to the newly converted Saul of Tarsus (Acts 9) and years later when Paul arrived in Ephesus (Acts 19). "It is illogical and unscriptural to tell a Christian that he has to do this or that in order to be worthy to receive the Holy Spirit," he declared. "The people who tell seekers that they must clean up and get more righteous before they can receive the Holy Spirit are defeating the very thing they are trying to promote."

Instead, Stiles encouraged believers to focus on the fact that a gracious God has already poured out His Spirit as a *gift*—and they have only to welcome it. He reminded them that the Spirit is like *breath* or *wind* (the Greek word *pneuma* can mean all three words in English). He talked about Jesus' use of this metaphor with the inquiring Nicodemus (John 3:8) . . . His action on Easter Night with the eleven disciples when "he breathed on them and said, 'Receive the Holy Spirit'" (John 20:22) . . . the "sound like the blowing of a violent wind [that] came from heaven" (Acts 2:2) on the Day of Pentecost.

At the end of a teaching session, Stiles would invite people to come sit quietly on the front pew and simply open their mouths to *breathe in* the Spirit of God. Very practically, he would say, "Don't utter a word in English. Don't say 'Jesus!' or 'Hallelujah!' or any other religious term; after all, you can't speak two languages at once. Just breathe in, and when the Spirit begins to put syllables upon your tongue, go ahead and give voice to them." He would then go down the row laying hands on each head as the apostles did, and within minutes the church would be filled with praises in altogether new vocabularies.

He probably wasn't aware that, decades earlier, Smith Wigglesworth (see chapter 2) had done the same thing. He had refused to call them "tarrying meetings" as others did. Instead he called them "receiving meetings." Said he: "You don't tarry for the Holy Ghost. He has already been given; He is here. You don't tarry, you receive." His biographer added, "'I will count to five,' he would say. 'When I get to five, then do as I have told you to do.' When he reached five, people would begin speaking in tongues. It was like waves rolling throughout the place."[1]

This fresh new (or old?) approach gradually became a centerpiece of Stiles's ministry, to the point that he resigned his pastorate in 1946 to start accepting the many invitations to come minister as an itinerant. He began to write on the subject, publishing a book of his teachings entitled *The Gift of the Holy Spirit*. His wife tried to keep track of how many people received the Holy Spirit in his meetings until, once she passed ten thousand, she gave up.

Defenders of the "tarrying" tradition, however, were not always happy with Stiles rocking their boat. His denomination brought him up for disciplinary hearings more than once. When, in early 1951, he traveled to Texas, his nephew invited him to speak to a class he was teaching at one of the denomination's ministry schools. Curiously, the nephew's teaching contract for the next year was not renewed.

But Stiles never voiced a criticism of his roots. He kept his credentials up-to-date, and the leaders chose not to disfellowship him. From coast to coast across the United States and Canada as well, he continued to go wherever the doors opened, whether denominational or independent churches. He and his wife purchased a simple travel trailer and stayed on the road until his stroke in 1957 forced them to retire. He passed away two years later.

Stiles's approach, though radical at the time, became far more mainstream as the charismatic movement swelled after his death. The laying on of hands has brought the Spirit's release to vast numbers of Christians around the world, for the benefit of God's Church. The bigger picture comes clear in what he wrote: "We are here to receive a Person, and not just an experience. The receiving of the Holy Spirit is only learning the first simple lesson in cooperating with the moving of the Holy Spirit in our lives."[2]

10

Donald Gee
(1891–1966)

The Apostle of Balance

Any movement sparked by strong visionaries and fiery preachers needs steady, clearheaded compatriots to keep the ship on an even keel.

Never would young Donald Gee have imagined such a role when he, at the age of fourteen, gave his heart to Christ in a London church. The guest preacher that day was a Methodist preacher who had been quite effective during the Welsh Revival—but on this occasion, only three hearers responded to his salvation call. The boy had already lost his father five years earlier to tuberculosis; now he would have a heavenly Father to guide him. And only God knew what He had in mind for this future influential churchman, respected author and educator who would write more than thirty books and hundreds of articles.

He was Spirit-baptized in his early twenties under the ministry of a Baptist-turned-Pentecostal pastor whom he revered as a "shining example of his office." Though earning his living as a sign painter (like his father), Gee soon began testifying, then preaching. On the recommendation of his mentor, he went with his wife and two young children to pastor a startup church in Edinburgh, Scotland. Its growth over the next twelve years put him in contact with such leaders as the Jeffreys brothers (Elim Pentecostal Church founders) and Smith Wigglesworth.

At the age of thirty, Gee ventured across the English Channel to attend the International Pentecostal Conference in Amsterdam, where his circle of acquaintances widened further. Three years later, he was invited to come teach in Australia and New Zealand; on the long voyage there, he wrote his first book, *Concerning Spiritual Gifts*. He played a leading role at the European Pentecostal Conference in Stockholm (1939) and, after World War II, organized a similar gathering in Zurich in 1947 with his South African friend David du Plessis. It was at this meeting that he was appointed editor of *Pentecost* magazine, which became his platform for the rest of his life.

Not everyone in Pentecostal ranks was thrilled with his open spirit; he took criticism, for example, when he cooperated with the tradition-shattering 1954 Billy Graham crusade in London's Harringay Arena. More flak came when Gee attended a World Council of Churches' Faith and Order Commission meeting in Scotland in 1960. Gee was not intimidated; he saw the Holy Spirit as a gift to the whole Church, not just one slice of it. Neither skepticism from inside nor outside the movement deterred him.

When charismatic renewal began to bubble up in Europe and North America, he gave it his encouragement, along with wise counsel. People on both continents began to call him the "apostle of balance." We can catch his nuances in an editorial entitled "Pentecost Is for All," where he started with a clever back-and-forth:

> "It's all right for your type of personality, but not for me." That remark, carrying a rather dubious compliment in its tone, was given as a reason why a fellow-Christian should take no interest in the baptism in the Holy Spirit or any matters classed under the heading "Pentecostal."
>
> His idea was that such matters involve a certain kind of emotionalism, and he prided himself as being one to whom that is foreign.
>
> He may not have been entirely to blame for his mistaken idea; perhaps we have stressed the emotional side a bit heavily. And admittedly some folk do go to extremes—even good ones.
>
> Of course, the truth is that in the very nature of the case the baptism in the Holy Spirit must be for every Christian, irrespective of temperament or upbringing or culture or any incident of personality. . . . A significantly recurrent word in the Bible story of Pentecost is *all*. "They were *all* in one accord." "They were *all* filled." "The promise is unto *all*" (Acts 2:1, 4, 39). There were no exceptions. . . .
>
> Rightly understood it involves far more than anything temperamental or denominational or sectarian or parochial. . . . It is God coming into the life in a fuller way.[1]

And Donald Gee, despite his British reserve and careful thought processing, was the kind of leader who made room for Holy Spirit surprises along the way. He was not afraid of bold strokes if they were God-ordained. He didn't want to settle down into a mushy middle ground that would avoid offending anyone.

We rightly extol the importance of balance; we correctly affirm that the way of truth will not be found in extremes; we justly point out that persistent extremism is suicidal both for men and movements—but we desperately need to recognize that revivals are never launched without someone going to an extreme. Passionate intercession is positively unbalanced; so is much fasting; so is fervent preaching that makes sinners tremble. . . .

The Day of Pentecost so disturbed the emotional balance of the disciples that they seemed like drunken men. . . . Thirty years later a Roman governor accused Paul of being mad. . . . There HAS to be an extremism to move things. . . . Miracles of healing occur when faith refuses to be logical, and blinds itself to arguments, based on plenty of contrary experience and more "balanced" teaching. . . .

So what was Gee's conclusion?

I can only reply that we need the extremist to start things moving, but we need the balanced teacher to keep them moving in the right direction. . . . Only a wisdom from above can reveal the perfect synthesis.[2]

History will forever appreciate the role he played as a teacher and mentor well into the 1960s. He helped many a younger enthusiast stay true to the Word without quenching the Spirit.

11

Agnes Sanford
(1897–1982)

Wholeness for Body and Mind

She lived in a comfortable New Jersey rectory with a loving husband and their three adorable young children—and she was miserable. The women of century-old Trinity Episcopal Church had welcomed her pleasantly, albeit with a bit of East Coast reserve. It was all so different from her growing-up years as the daughter of Presbyterian missionaries in China . . . or even her post-college seasons of teaching English there. In troubled moments, she remembered a certain missionary wife who had struggled silently with depression and ended up taking her own life. Surely this would not be her fate, would it?

"The kind of person that I used to be was dead," she wrote later. "And the new person, whom I was now forced to be, had much trouble in living."[1] Even the need to prepare three meals a day for her family was burdensome because she considered herself a terrible cook.

"I wanted to be a writer, and I could not, for all of my time and thought and attention was upon being a wife and mother. . . . For many months I could not go near an upstairs window without wondering when I would throw myself out of it. . . . I seldom peeled vegetables without wondering whether the kitchen knife was sharp enough. . . .

"My doctor said [later] that he had not thought I would last another year."[2]

At one point, her youngest child, eighteen-month-old Jack, developed an ear infection that would not go away. He ran a fever for six weeks. One day a nearby Episcopal priest, Hollis Colwell, stopped by to visit the Sanfords, and upon hearing of the child's condition, offered to go up to the nursery and pray for him. Agnes said that would be rather pointless, since her little son was too young to understand. Colwell replied that it didn't matter, because God would understand.

Proceeding up the stairs, he laid his hands on the whimpering child's head and prayed a quiet prayer. To the mother's amazement, Jack calmed down and drifted off into a nap. When he awakened an hour or two later, the fever was gone and he was happy again. Agnes Sanford couldn't believe it.

On a Sunday morning not long afterward, as her depression continued, she was at the altar rail to receive Communion when she heard a distinct voice: *Go to Hollis Colwell and ask him to pray for you.* Twenty-four hours later, she was in the priest's office, where he asked a few questions and then proceeded to lay hands on her and pray. He had hardly finished when, she said, "Great waves of joy flooded my mind." The dark cloud had vanished. The following days and months confirmed that a genuine miracle had taken place.

She immediately began to tell anyone who would listen what had set her free after six years of gloom. If any woman of the parish confided to her an emotional or physical struggle, she sent her to Hollis Colwell. In time, the traffic became so much that Colwell said she needed to start praying for the sick herself. Healing wasn't restricted to the ordained clergy, he said; anyone with faith in an omnipotent God could ask and receive His intervention.

And that was the beginning of a half-century of ministry for Agnes Sanford. She never sought to speak to large audiences or become a public personality. She ministered most often to people one at a time, either because they came to her, or because she went where the need was obvious—hospitals, for example, especially veterans' hospitals during World War II.

Colwell had also advised her to make time for her gift of writing. In fact, he prescribed that she dedicate two hours each morning, once her children had been fed and sent off to school, to go over to the parish house and start putting words to paper. Her first book, *The Healing Light*, finally appeared in 1947 and became a perennial bestseller, going through 35 printings in hardcover and then on to paperback. It inspired readers to see a God who truly cared about their infirmities and would lovingly act. The book was chockful of examples, such as:

I went to see a little girl who had been in a cast for five months following infantile paralysis [polio]. One day I placed my hands above the rigid knee in that instinctive laying-on of hands that every mother knows. . . . And I asked that the light of God might shine through me into the small, stiff knee and make it well.

"Oh, take your hands away!" cried the little girl. "It's hot."

"That's God's power working in your knee, Sally," I replied. "It's like electricity working in your lamp. I guess it has to be hot, so as to make the knee come back to life. So you just stand it now for a few minutes, while I tell you about Peter Rabbit."

By the time the erring Peter had returned home without his shoes and his new red jacket and had been put to bed with castor oil, the pulsation of energy in my hands had died away.

"Now crawl out to the edge of the bed, Sally, and see if that leg will bend," I directed the child.

She pulled herself to the edge of the bed and sat up. And the leg that had been rigid [now] bent at an angle of forty-five degrees. Within two weeks she was walking.

"How do you turn on God's electricity in your hands?" she asked me at my next visit.

"I don't turn it on," I replied. "I just forget everything else and think about God and about Jesus, who is God's Son and our friend. And I believe that God can turn on that light in me because Jesus said He could. He turns it on, and when He is through with it, He turns it off."

Sally and I both understood quite simply that God's life was a kind of light.[3]

When in the early 1950s some friends wrote to Agnes about receiving the baptism in the Holy Spirit, she agreed to let them pray for her as well. As a result, she was filled with the Spirit and spoke in tongues. She hesitated for a long time to tell her husband what had happened, knowing that their denomination would not (at that time) be receptive. But eventually the truth came out, and no harm ensued.

She and her supportive husband eventually set up the School of Pastoral Care, a vehicle to minister to hurting pastors, and also to teach them how to care for others in the same way. This effort eventually spread beyond the United States to other nations around the world.

She became what some today call the "mother" of the inner-healing movement, which treated painful memories with prayer, forgiveness, repentance and the rejection of long-held lies so that divine truth could take their place.

Her writings continued with more than twenty books published by major firms (J. B. Lippincott, Harper & Row), including such titles as *The Healing Gifts of the Spirit, The Healing Power of the Bible* and her autobiography, *Sealed Orders*. She held steadfast in her confidence in a God who loves His children enough to relieve and restore them, if only we humans would be His willing channels. Her website today includes this frank assessment:

> She said Jesus stood in church services all over Christendom with his hands tied behind his back because neither ministers nor people expected him to do anything. She said people who prayed had to expect miracles. That required them to pray down the voice of doubt within them based on old hurts, griefs, and failures. "There is more in the Bible than mere information. A spiritual energy we call faith seems to connect with the very book itself."[4]

To those who wondered if she might be overstating her case in light of Paul's "thorn in the flesh" (2 Corinthians 12:7), she wrote in *The Healing Light*:

> St. Paul's thorn in the flesh has become a veritable thorn in the spirit to thousands of Christians, who take St. Paul as an example for cherishing illness. In this they are not consistent. If St. Paul were really their example, they could raise the dead. For in seeing him as an example of the invalid saint, they do the utmost violence to the Biblical pattern of a man strong enough to endure shipwreck and exposure, stoning and imprisonment and still accomplish more than ten ordinary men could. . . .

[Granted,] he did not receive an instantaneous healing. Instead of that, he received everyday enough of the Grace of God for that day's needs. So do I. And if God's perfect strength accomplished as much through me as it did through St. Paul, I would be well content.[5]

12

Leo Josef Suenens
(1904–1996)

The Charismatic Cardinal

U nder a blazing June sun, some 25,000 expectant Catholic charismatics in the University of Notre Dame's football stadium kept watching the tunnel from which the Fighting Irish usually charged onto the field—but not this day. Instead, two long lines of priests in white robes and clerical stoles emerged, more than six hundred in all. The applause swelled into a roar as the procession climaxed with eight bishops and then, in his unmistakable blood-red garb, a Belgian prince of the church appointed by the pope himself: Cardinal Leo Josef Suenens. "Alleluia! Alleluia!" sang the throng.

This celebration in 1973—an annual event over several decades—swelled throughout the morning with prayers, exhortations and prophetic utterances. When His Eminence approached the podium, he said, "The gifts of the Spirit are given specially to build up the Christian community. After Vatican II, we had to make a series of reforms, and we must continue to do so. But it is not enough to change the body. We need to change the soul to renew the Church."[1]

Many in the crowd that day knew the crucial role he had played a decade earlier at Vatican II, the groundbreaking council that revised liturgical prayers, shortened the liturgical calendar, let nuns modernize their clothing and allowed the mass to be celebrated in current languages, not just Latin. Cardinal Suenens was a key player throughout the sessions, serving as one of four moderators and arguing convincingly that the gifts of the Spirit were not just for ancient times.

One memorable moment happened on October 22, 1963, when a senior Italian cardinal expressed his view that any charismatic gifts should be limited to the clergy. The Belgian openly intervened. "These special gifts of the Holy Spirit to the Church do exist today," he declared, and should not be fenced off. "Without the shepherds, the Church would be undisciplined; but without the charisms, it would be sterile. Therefore, the pastors must heed the warnings of St. Paul and take care not to 'stifle the Spirit.'"[2]

Obviously, he had been listening to Pope John XXIII's prayer each day, "Renew thy wonders in this our day as by a new Pentecost." This was all part of the council's theme of badly needed *aggiornamento* ("updating").

The next pope, Paul VI, continued the work begun, although he worried that the charismatic movement "is very risky, because it advances into a field in which auto-suggestion, or the influence of imponderable, psychical causes, can lead to spiritual error." But he trusted Suenens, appointing him the papal liaison to Catholic charismatics worldwide.

Reporters wanted to know whether the dignified cardinal with the slicked-back hair actually spoke in tongues himself. After all, his official coat of arms carried the motto *In Spiritu Sancto* ("In the Holy Spirit"). He artfully dodged the question by saying that his own spiritual life was "too delicate" for public spotlighting. He pulled back the curtain a bit more in his 1975 book *A New Pentecost?* by writing:

> I did not discover the Holy Spirit through the Renewal. As I have said, the Spirit had long been at the center of my life. . . . I saw how some Christians live, who took the Acts of the Apostles at its word, and this led me to question the depth and genuineness of my own faith. As a result, I found that I believed in the action of the Holy Spirit, but in a limited sphere; in me the Spirit could not call forth from the organ all the melody he wished; some of the pipes did not function, because they had not been used.[3]

From that point on, he welcomed the life-giving energy that an unshackled Spirit could release. He was astute enough to admit that Pentecostals sometimes veered into excesses. "When you light a lamp in the darkness," he observed, "you will draw some mosquitoes." But that did not dissuade him. He added that the renewal was "not a movement. It is a current of grace . . . growing fast everywhere in the world. I feel it coming, and I see it coming."[4]

Ever the loyal churchman, he convened a weeklong gathering of Catholic theologians and renewal leaders in 1974 to the archbishop's house in Malines (outside Brussels) to undergird and clarify the charismatic phenomenon. The six resulting "Malines Documents," as they are called, dealt with everything from how Catholics should understand the term "baptism in the Holy Spirit" to social action to exorcism to relations with likeminded non-Catholics. The first document, entitled "Theological and Pastoral Orientations on the Catholic Charismatic Renewal," was largely Suenens's work. These papers are still respected today; Pope Francis said as recently as 2014, "In the Malines Documents, you have a guide, a reliable path to keep you from going astray."

To guard against problems, Suenens decreed at one point that prayer groups across his archdiocese needed to be led by priests rather than freelance laity, who might be tempted toward error or separation. Yet he could never be accused of squelching the flow of the Spirit. He wanted to see the renewal remain a gift to the entire Church.

His successor in Belgium described him later as an excellent weather forecaster, in that he always seemed to know which way the wind was blowing in the Church, and how he should adjust the sails to suit it. When he finally died at the age of 91, his obituary in the *New York Times* called him "a major architect of 20th-century Roman Catholicism."[5] Those who had heard him that summer day at Notre Dame could still recall his strong voice echoing across the stadium, "You are in such a special way the people of God."[6] And so was he.

13

David du Plessis
(1905–1987)

The Bridge Builder

I n the spring of 1960, a Methodist bishop and twenty of his superintendents and officials sat together in a room to meet a very different kind of clergyman: David Johannes du Plessis (pronounced *DU-pleh-see*). Now living in the United States, he had spent the first four decades of life in his native South Africa, where sharp lines were drawn not only between blacks and whites (such as himself), but just as firmly between mainline denominations and upstart Pentecostal groups.

His hosts that day, however, "had a definite experience of salvation," he wrote. "The great complaint was a 'powerless ministry' and 'churches that are spiritually dead.' As I sat where they sat, I was astonished to hear the humble confessions of men that hunger for a real heaven-sent Holy Spirit

Revival. Such contrition cannot go without the reward of the Lord."

Du Plessis spoke with clarity about the work of the Spirit, using such words as "The New Testament is not a record of what happened in one generation, but it is a blueprint of what should happen in every generation, until Jesus comes. Every generation must be regenerated by the Spirit." Questions soon flowed freely, and responses were shared. The last question of the day was perhaps the most telling: "Why is it that you are the only Pentecostal we have yet found that will come to us in love and show such an interest in our spiritual welfare?"

Du Plessis frankly admitted that ten years earlier, even he would not have joined such a meeting. In his autobiography, *The Spirit Bade Me Go*, he told about a similar gathering in Connecticut:

> I could remember days when I had wished I could have set my eyes upon such men to denounce their theology and pray the judgment of God upon them for what I considered their heresies and false doctrines. . . . [But] after a few introductory words, I suddenly felt a warm glow come over me. I knew this was the Holy Spirit taking over, but, what was He doing to me? Instead of the old harsh spirit of criticism and condemnation in my heart, I now felt such love and compassion for these ecclesiastical leaders that I would rather have died for them than pass sentence upon them.[1]

He had been notified as early as 1936, by a bold prophecy from British evangelist Smith Wigglesworth, that this change of ministry focus would come. (To read the account, see chapter 2.) Following World War II, he had helped bring various Pentecostal groups together in world conferences (Zurich 1947,

Paris 1949, London 1952). But when he had reached out to the Presbyterian president of Princeton Theological Seminary, John Alexander Mackay, about some critical remarks the man had made about Latin American Pentecostals, du Plessis was kindly received—and soon invited to an upcoming meeting of the International Missionary Council in Germany. There he met dozens of traditional leaders and was even asked to speak. It was the beginning of his presence at many World Council of Churches (WCC) events.

Soon he was giving lectures at such major seminaries as Yale, Union, and Princeton. His listeners started calling him "Mr. Pentecost." At the WCC's Commission on Faith and Order meeting in St. Andrews, Scotland, in August 1960, he was the Friday night speaker, tracing the rise of the worldwide Pentecostal movement but also quoting several reputable mainline scholars in his appeal for interaction, not isolation.

He chose his words carefully; for example, he often spoke about tongues as a *consequence* or *confirmation* of the Spirit's infilling, rather than the harder-edged term *evidence* used in many Pentecostal statements of faith. His bridge-building made some of his fellow Pentecostals nervous, as they recalled the expulsions their forefathers had endured by some of the churches du Plessis was now befriending. In 1961, the National Association of Evangelicals magazine called on him to back away from this work; after all, its current president was none other than the general superintendent of the Assemblies of God—the body with which du Plessis held ordination.

He prayed about the matter and sought counsel. When the next year the Assemblies asked him to surrender his credentials, he quietly complied. (The denomination reversed itself on this in 1980.) Wherever he went, he advised mainstream colleagues to keep being a voice for Spirit-filled life in their present environments. He told an interviewer from Fuller Theological Seminary:

> I had . . . met James Brown, a Presbyterian, who wanted to know from me what Pentecostal group I would suggest he join. I said, "Stay in your church, because I believe I have a very clear assignment from the Lord never to invite anybody out of his or her church or suggest any change of churches. Stay in your church. God is going to do a wonderful thing. . . ."
>
> Later, I got a letter from [Episcopalian rector] Dennis Bennett saying, "I . . . am in a very difficult position here. The [Van Nuys, California] church is in danger of splitting. I can split the church or form a new society, or I can ask the Bishop to give me another assignment."
>
> I said to him, "Don't split the church. Every speckled bird in the area will join you and you'll have an impossible congregation. Nobody will trust you. Stay in the church and ask the Bishop for another appointment." That's how Dennis Bennett found a challenge in Seattle.[2]

He believed with all his heart that "to be Pentecostal you have to be ecumenical, and to remain Pentecostal you have to be ecumenical. . . . You cannot create unity. You cannot organize unity. But you must expect unity to come about by a creation of the Holy Spirit."[3]

Thanks to his gracious temperament, du Plessis was invited by a Catholic cardinal to attend the third session of Vatican II. He helped a Benedictine monk (Fr. Killian McDonnell) put together the International Roman Catholic-Pentecostal Dialogue and served as its co-chair for its first ten sessions. Over the years, he was given audiences with three different popes (John XXIII, Paul VI and John Paul II). In 1983, the pope bestowed upon him the golden Benemerenti ("Good Merit") medal for excellent "service to all Christianity." He was the first non-Catholic in history to receive this honor.

Whenever worried Protestants would ask him how he could countenance the veneration of Mary, the white-haired gentleman would smile and say in his delightful South African accent, "I try to remember what Mary said to the servants at the wedding in Cana. Motioning toward her Son, she said, 'Whatsoever he saith unto you, do it'" (John 2:5 KJV). If all Christians of all persuasions were to follow that directive, du Plessis reasoned, we would do well.

14

Gordon & Freda Lindsay

(1906–1973) / (1914–2010)

Making Connections

Close your eyes and envision yourself back in 1951 . . . your eight-year-old daughter has just awakened crying for the fifth night this month. "My head hurts!" she moans as you hold her close and gently rub her curly scalp. *What is going on inside there?!* you worry, imagining the worst. You've already taken her to your family doctor, who hesitates to put her through the risks of an X-ray.

Oh, Lord, help me know what to do, you silently plead. You remember reading in the Bible "how God anointed Jesus of Nazareth with the Holy Ghost and with power: who went about doing good, and healing all that were oppressed of the devil; for

God was with him" (Acts 10:38 KJV). But you've never heard a sermon on that text, nor seen anyone pray directly for the sick.

Then a friend at church shows you a slim magazine she has just discovered. Its name: *The Voice of Healing*. You ask to borrow it so you can read articles with titles such as "Bible Preaching Brings Bible Results" and testimonies of dramatic miracles ("Girl with Severed Vocal Cords Sings over Radio"). On one page you notice a directory of upcoming campaigns led by various healing evangelists across the nation—Richard Vinyard, A. C. Valdez, W. V. Grant, William Branham, Oral Roberts. In fact, one of them will be coming to a city less than 150 miles away. Should you take your daughter?

Suddenly, you don't feel quite so alone.

In that era before the Internet, social media or even Christian television channels, the word would not have spread nearly so widely without the efforts of Gordon and Freda Lindsay. They had met while he was preaching tent revivals up and down the West Coast, eventually getting married and settling down to pastor a church in southern Oregon. One day in March 1947, just as they were wrapping up a series of meetings with Evangelist J. E. Stiles in which some fifty people had been baptized in the Holy Spirit (see chapter 9), a letter arrived from a fellow minister they knew. He told of healings taking place in Oakland, California, "on such a scale as I have never seen before," led by a still-obscure evangelist named William Branham. He urged Gordon to travel the three hundred miles south and see for himself.

The Lindsays read the letter slowly several times "with mingled emotions," he later wrote, "and finally took it and read it to Brother Stiles. His own spirit witnessed with us on the matter, and we both determined to make the trip down. . . ."[1] The first night's service was more than enough to establish credibility. In an appointment the next morning, it was agreed for Gordon, who held Assemblies of God credentials, to help introduce Branham to wider circles of ministry friends. In the coming months, Gordon traveled to Tulsa and then Calgary to observe Branham's ministry, where deaf ears were instantly opened, crossed eyes straightened and wheelchairs emptied. By the end of the year, he had taken a leave of absence from his pastorate to become the evangelist's campaign manager.

And so began the Lindsays' unique role as information source, advocate and networker of the healing surge throughout the 1950s and beyond. *The Voice of Healing,* begun in April 1948 to publicize Branham's events, soon began to carry news of other itinerant ministries. Gordon wrote news reports and editorials for every issue; he selected articles by various evangelists to help explain "the great truth of Divine Healing, but not to the exclusion of other great evangelical truths of the Scriptures."[2] Subscriptions ($1 per year) rose briskly. People across the continent wanted to know what was happening in this fresh outpouring of healing power, and Gordon Lindsay was the one to tell them.

Coverage eventually expanded even to foreign crusades such as those led by Tommy Hicks (especially in Argentina) and T. L. Osborn (in more than forty countries). By 1956, the Voice of Healing organization was sending out its own teams to evangelize across the world. As converts in poor areas gathered into congregations, the Lindsays' "Native Church Crusade" helped them put up simple structures—no strings attached. American donors were asked to pay for the roofs for these buildings; some 12,800 roofs were provided altogether.

His entrepreneurial skills were evident in starting a Dallas printing plant to produce not only the magazine but also his books (some 250 in all) and other materials. (That plant eventually relocated, under the leadership of son Gilbert Lindsay, to the unlikely Eastern European site of Minsk, Belarus, where it continues today to export huge quantities of Bibles and books under the name World Wide Printing.)

The international focus went public more than ever when the organization name was changed to Christ For The Nations. To train more young workers for global outreach, a new Bible college opened in 1970 in Dallas, tagging itself as the "home of adventurers, revivalists, and passionate worshippers of Jesus."[3] Gordon Lindsay poured heart and soul into this launch for three years, until suddenly, during a Sunday afternoon worship service, while Freda stood speaking at the podium, he slumped in his chair behind her—and was gone at age sixty-six.

For the next three decades, she and her son Dennis picked up Gordon's mantle and led Christ For The Nations Institute to great growth. Its course credits in missions, counseling, creative media and other subjects have been accepted by such institutions as Oral Roberts University and Dallas Baptist University. Its eight hundred full-time students enjoy an impressive ninety-acre campus. In addition, another 5,300 are enrolled in the 91 members of the CFNI Association of Bible Schools across 46 countries.

Freda's life, and that of her husband as well, can be summarized in what she wrote in her book *Fire in His Bones*: "If you stay humble before God, giving Him all the glory, and keep up your prayer life and study of the Word, the whole world will hear of your faith and your exploits."

15

Kathryn Kuhlman
(1907–1976)

Daughter of Destiny

If you were hunting for cracks in the reputation of Kathryn Kuhlman, you would not have to look far:

She had almost no formal theological training.

She was a *woman* who nevertheless preached openly to huge audiences, in an era when such activity was usually censured.

She, at age thirty-one, brushed aside all wise counsel to marry a recently divorced evangelist with two sons, which alienated many of her followers. This marriage dissolved in less than ten years.

Her only ordination was from an obscure group with no congregations of its own and no follow-up system for oversight.

She repeatedly fibbed about her age, brushing it aside as a "woman's prerogative."

Her speaking style was ultra-dramatic, with mid-sentence pauses and stretched-out vowels as she enunciated *the great and marvelous—good news!—of God's ama-a-a-zing—miracle power—through the touch—of the—Ho-o-o-o-ly Spirit!* The throngs who packed her meetings seemed mesmerized by her delivery, while many others found it distracting and artificial; one nationally syndicated columnist termed it "unbelievable corn."

In summary, Kathryn Kuhlman was easy to discount. Several writers have belittled her as a high-school dropout—although that is not true; in the small Missouri town where she grew up, the high school only went up through grade ten, which she completed. She quickly headed northwest to help her older sister and husband in their "sawdust trail" tent meetings, where she got her first speaking opportunities. Eventually she and a pianist friend, Helen Gulliford, struck out on their own, holding services from town to town, until finally arriving in Denver in 1933 to open the Kuhlman Revival Tabernacle (later renamed the Denver Revival Tabernacle).

Her message in those years was not about healing; it was a straightforward appeal for salvation. Crowds flocked in seven nights a week to hear the tall young woman in the flowing dress and the Shirley Temple hairdo as she urged them to get right with God. Both the chief of police and the city fire chief responded to her altar calls.

But it all imploded in the wake of her ill-advised marriage to Burroughs Waltrip, and she went quiet until after World War II. She gradually resumed preaching in various tabernacles, and on a Monday night in Franklin, Pennsylvania, a fiftyish woman came down the aisle just as Kathryn was about to begin her message, asking to say something. "Last night, while you were preaching, I was healed," she claimed.

"Where were you?" Kuhlman asked.

"Just sitting here in the audience . . . I had a tumor. It had been diagnosed by my doctor. While you were preaching, something happened in my body. I was so sure I was healed that I went back to my doctor this morning and had it verified. The tumor is no longer there."

There had been no focus on healing the night before. Kathryn Kuhlman was as surprised as anyone. But God had silently done a miracle.

The next Sunday morning, as she preached about the Holy Spirit's power, a Methodist man who had suffered an industrial accident that left him legally blind and drawing workman's compensation suddenly had tears streaming from his eyes. He could not stop the watering. On the ride home, he kept blinking—and then shouting, "I can see! I can see everything!"

By 1948, Kathryn Kuhlman had relocated down the highway to Pittsburgh, which was to be her headquarters for the rest of her ministry. Her services at Carnegie Hall and First Presbyterian Church, complete with a massive choir, became famous not only for her messages but for her unique declarations that such-and-such a disease was being healed over in the right section . . . a different disease on the left . . . still another in the balcony. She did not call the sick to form a line for her prayers as other evangelists did (in fact, she had been appalled at seeing that method in a tent revival in Erie). She simply announced what God was already doing and invited people to come to the platform and describe it.

Redbook magazine ran a seven-page feature on her ministry. By 1965, she began holding once-a-month healing services on the West Coast, first in Pasadena's Civic Auditorium and then, to gain more space, in the Los Angeles Shrine Auditorium (seating: seven thousand). She would be on her feet four to five hours at a time. She launched two TV programs, *Your Faith and Mine* and *I Believe in Miracles* (or, as she would exude at the start of every taping, "I *beee-LEEEEve* in miracles!"). Eventually she was racking up five hundred thousand air miles a year.

Did people actually receive permanent healing, as opposed to just temporary remissions? Some two million claimed so. When *Time* magazine ran a piece on her in 1970, calling her "a veritable one-woman shrine of Lourdes," it included four examples with names, places and doctors' verifications: a twelve-year-old's rheumatoid arthritis, a seven-year-old's severely deteriorated eardrum, a twenty-nine-year-old woman's calcified tendon in her left elbow and a sixty-nine-year-old woman's lymphatic leukemia.[1]

Equally dramatic were the reactions of those who came forward to testify of being made well: Scores of them fell backward "under the power" at the soft touch of her hand—or even before she touched them. Was this autosuggestion? Did this woman employ some kind of hypnotic power, as *Tonight Show* host Johnny Carson once speculated? Or was this truly a work of God's power, like what happened in Bible times to King Saul (1 Samuel 19:23–24), the prophet Ezekiel (Ezekiel 1:28–2:1) or the apostle Paul (Acts 9:4 and 26:14)? She did not try to analyze.

While some of those who collapsed were no doubt susceptible to going along with the rest, that would not explain what her biographer Jamie Buckingham witnessed in her backstage room at the end of an LA meeting. She was clearly exhausted . . . until a knock came at the door. Waiting outside was none other than war hero and five-star General of the Army Omar Bradley, who had attended the service. This tough-as-nails, battle-hardened warrior said he wanted her to intercede for a specific need in his life.

"Dear Jesus," Kathryn intoned, closing her eyes and reaching out to pray for him.

It was as far as she got. His legs buckled under him and he crumpled backwards—"slain in the Spirit." Don Barnard, who traveled with Miss Kuhlman as her bodyguard, had entered the room with the general. He caught him as he fell and eased him to the floor where he lay for a few moments as if he were asleep. When he began to move slightly, Don helped him to his feet and gently held his arm. He was still unsteady.

"Our wonderful Lord can meet your every need," Kathryn said deliberately, her face glowing with faith. "I know how much He must love you right this minute."

She made no more move in his direction, but the general's knees buckled once again and he slipped back into Don's strong arms.[2]

Kathryn Kuhlman will be remembered, in the words of Duke Divinity School historian Grant Wacker, as "one of the key figures to transform the 'down-home' Pentecostal revival of the early 20th century into the 'uptown' charismatic movement of the late 20th century."[3] She broke the molds of Pentecostals and non-Pentecostals alike. This is her legacy, far more than what another biographer (Amy Artman of Missouri State University) described as "her flair for style and a little 'sass' in her choice of white high-heeled ankle-strap shoes that showed off her long legs to good advantage."[4]

When she was asked—hundreds of times—why everyone was not healed in her meetings, she did not pontificate. She said that was the first question she would ask when she got to heaven. "The only answer I can give," she wrote, "is: I do not know. And I am afraid of those who claim they know. For only God knows, and who can fathom the mind of God? . . . Only Jesus can work the work that will lift us to the mountain peaks of victory."

16

Leonard Ravenhill

(1907–1994)

Sounding the Alarm

Long before the birth of Twitter in 2006, the British-American author and revivalist Leonard Ravenhill was framing serious soundbites of truth that would have made great tweets. A few of them:

The only reason we don't have revival is because we are willing to live without it.

Men give advice; God gives guidance.

My main ambition in life is to be on the Devil's Most-Wanted List.

Ravenhill's unique talent for arresting people's attention was honed over thirty years in the towns and villages of his native England, where he began preaching soon after finishing his studies at a Methodist school called Cliff College. There, under the tutelage of the Holiness exponent Samuel Chadwick, his heart had burned early to see genuine revival. He and his Irish wife, Martha, brought that passion across the Atlantic when they moved in 1958 to Minneapolis, settling at Bethany College of Missions.

The next year, when Bethany's publishing arm released his first book, *Why Revival Tarries*, it shocked many in the Christian world. Take for example the very first paragraph:

> The Cinderella of the church of today is the prayer meeting. This handmaid of the Lord is unloved and unwooed because she is not dripping with the pearls of intellectualism, nor glamorous with the silks of philosophy; neither is she enchanting with the tiara of psychology. She wears the homespuns of sincerity and humility and so is not afraid to kneel![1]

By page four, he was declaring:

> The ugly fact is that altar fires are either out or burning very low. . . . By our attitude to prayer we tell God that what was begun in the Spirit we can finish in the flesh. What church ever asks its candidating ministers what time they spend in prayer? Yet ministers who do not spend two hours a day in prayer are not worth a dime a dozen, degrees or no degrees.[2]

And this at the end of the 1950s—a decade viewed by many today as a high point in American evangelicalism!

Ravenhill was not impressed with full sanctuaries or flowery sermons. He had no time for flashy music or well-oiled church bureaucracy. He craved only the fire of God that brought sinners to repentance and believers to holy living. "A sinning man stops praying," he said, "a praying man stops sinning." He rankled more than a few clergy when he declared, "If Jesus had preached the same message that ministers preach today, He would never have been crucified."

No wonder A. W. Tozer, noted editor of the *Alliance Witness* magazine (which published many of Ravenhill's short articles), wrote in his foreword to *Why Revival Tarries:*

> Toward Leonard Ravenhill it is impossible to be neutral. His acquaintances are divided pretty neatly into two classes, those who love and admire him out of all proportion and those who hate him with perfect hatred. And what is true of the man is sure to be true of his books, of this book. The reader will either close its pages to seek a place of prayer or he will toss it away in anger, his heart closed to its warnings and appeals.
>
> Not all books, not even good books come as a voice from above, but I feel that this one does.[3]

To the surprise of the Christian publishing establishment, the hard-hitting *Why Revival Tarries* sold more than a million copies.

Ravenhill told few anecdotes about his own ministry; he would rather quote John Wesley, David Brainerd, Charles Finney and E. M. Bounds. He crafted no long lectures on theology—Pentecostal or otherwise. Nevertheless, throughout the next three decades in America, Ravenhill influenced a wide array of future Christian leaders. Listen to Ravi Zacharias, for one: "The truth is, even though I am known now as an apologist for the Christian faith, dealing with the intellectual issues of Christianity, I really owe any passion for God, for prayer and for true revival that initially began in me, to Leonard Ravenhill. He, by God's grace, was the catalyst that has caused the passion to know God to continue to this day."[4]

David Wilkerson, the young Assemblies of God pastor who dared to go meet New York City gangbangers and tell them about Jesus (resulting in the ministry we know today as Teen

Challenge), said, "Leonard Ravenhill was one of the few men I have ever known who was a true prophet."[5]

Perhaps the most unusual linkage began in the 1980s, when the aging Ravenhills moved to Lindale, Texas, and began teaching young longhairs (among others) at Last Days Ministries. This was the headquarters of firebrand singer/songwriter Keith Green, who called Ravenhill "Papa." The Ravenhills opened their home for Friday night prayer meetings that went on for hours; one participant named Mark Dance (now a Southern Baptist executive) remembers, "He prayed with so much intensity that I expected the carpet under his knees to catch on fire."

Keith Green, of course, was at the top of the music charts in those years, crafting such songs as "Oh, Lord, You're Beautiful" and "So You Wanna Go Back to Egypt." He is enshrined today in the Gospel Music Hall of Fame. His serious passion for God was due in great measure to being mentored by the man with the British accent who was 46 years older than he. Some called them the Odd Couple of Revival. They are buried nearly side by side in Garden Valley, Texas, where the etching on Ravenhill's tombstone throws out one last challenge: "Are the things you are living for worth Christ dying for"?

(As for Keith Green: The Ravenhill influence bleeds through in the title of his biography, *No Compromise*—written by his widow, Melody, after his untimely death in a plane crash at the age of 28.)

Ravenhill claimed to have seen a church signboard back in England that read, "This church will have either a revival or a funeral!" He commented:

With such despair God is well pleased, though hell is despondent. Madness, you say? Exactly! A sober church never does any good. At this hour we need men drunk with the Holy Ghost. Has God excelled Himself? Were Wesley, Whitefield, Finney, Hudson Taylor special editions of ministers? Never! If I read the Book of Acts aright, they were just the norm.[6]

Leonard Ravenhill aspired to be no less.

17

William Branham
(1909–1965)
God's Nobody

I f you were playing the "Who Am I?" game with a classroom of fifth-graders, what answer would you get to these clues? *Born in the backwoods of Kentucky . . . in a log cabin with only a dirt floor . . . got very little schooling . . . worked hard to help raise crops in the clearing . . . while still a boy, had to move across the Ohio River to southern Indiana because his father had legal problems . . . but nevertheless grew up to make a great impact as an adult.*

Hands would quickly shoot up. "I know, I know! Abraham Lincoln!"

An equally valid answer, not from the world of politics but rather from spiritual history, would be William Branham. His early years of deprivation were so hard that he often was seen wearing a buttonless coat pinned together with safety pins, since there was no shirt underneath. His hauling of water from the spring was not only for his parents and nine younger siblings to drink and use for washing, but also to supply his father's whiskey-making still.

Unlike the Lincoln family, which acquired a Bible that young Abe read by firelight, the Branhams had no religious ties at all; the first time William heard a prayer was as a twenty-year-old at his brother's funeral.

So, how did God ever get through to him? The same way He got through to Noah, to Abraham, to Gideon, to the young Samuel, among others in ancient times—by direct speaking. As early as the age of three, the boy remembered hearing a "voice" from a nearby tree telling him that he would "live near a city called New Albany." (This came true decades later, when his ministry blossomed in neighboring Jeffersonville, Indiana; both towns lie across the river from Louisville, Kentucky.)

At the age of seven, another voice warned him always to stay away from cigarettes and alcohol (despite his father's negative example), "for there will be work for you to do when you get older." Finally, while working for the public utility company, an industrial accident filled his lungs with gas, almost killing him; during recovery, a voice led him to begin seeking God. He showed up at the First Pentecostal Baptist Church of Jeffersonville, where he was converted.

He grew rapidly in his faith, to the point that he was allowed to speak at times. By the next year, a group helped set up a tent for him to conduct revival meetings. The local newspaper reported fourteen converts. At a baptismal in the Ohio River on June 11, 1933, a bright star descended over him, and he heard a voice say, "As John the Baptist was sent to forerun the first coming of Jesus Christ, so your message will forerun His second coming." Soon a new church was organized, the

Branham Tabernacle, where he pastored for the next thirteen years, while continuing his job as a game warden. He married during that season and became the father of two children—only to lose his first wife (to tuberculosis) and their infant daughter just four days apart in 1937.

Branham remarried four years later and welcomed three more children. On May 4, 1946, he went away to a remote place to focus entirely on what God wanted for his future. About eleven o'clock that night . . .

> I heard someone walking across the floor, which startled me. . . . [Then] I saw the feet of a man coming toward me. . . . He appeared to be a man who, in human weight, would weigh about two hundred pounds, clothed in a white robe, had a smooth face, no beard, but with dark hair down to his shoulders, rather dark-complected, with a very pleasant countenance, and, coming closer, his eyes caught with mine, and seeing how fearful I was, he began to speak. "Fear not! I am sent from the presence of Almighty God to tell you that your peculiar life and your misunderstood ways have been to indicate that God has sent you to take a gift of divine healing to the peoples of the world. If you will be sincere, and can get the people to believe you, nothing shall stand before your prayer, not even cancer."
>
> He told me how I would be able to detect diseases by vibrations on my hand. He went away, but I have seen him a number of times since. . . . A few times he has appeared visibly in the presence of others. I do not know who he is, I only know that he is the messenger of God to me.[1]

Whatever doubts William Branham (or anyone else) may have harbored about this event, the angel's words quickly proved true. In St. Louis the next month, his twelve nights of meetings drew a crowd of more than four thousand and a story in *Time* magazine; historians today mark this as the birth of the post–World War II healing surge. Invitations came flooding in for him to come preach and pray for the sick. A Jonesboro, Arkansas, gathering in August drew 25,000 people from 28 different states. By the next year, he was off to Shreveport, Louisiana, then other more distant cities throughout the early 1950s: San Antonio, Phoenix, Kansas City, Vancouver. He insisted that his meetings, even in this segregated era, must always be interracial.

His preaching style was not flamboyant; he spoke in a normal tone of voice, even faltering at times. Yet people were inspired to believe that God could do any miracle. When he ended his message and began praying for the sick, the Spirit regularly gave him a word of knowledge about the individual in front of him. Said Ern Baxter, his campaign manager for seven years, "He would give accurate details concerning the person's ailments, and also details of their lives—their hometown, activities, actions—even way back in their childhood. Branham never once made a mistake with the word of knowledge in all the years I was with him. That covers, in my case, thousands of instances."[2] A similar report came later from Swiss theologian Walter J. Hollenweger, who was his translator during Zurich meetings and said he was "not aware of any case in which he was mistaken in the often detailed statements he made."[3]

Branham, unlike other evangelists who soon began holding their own services, did not minister to long healing lines on the platform; he normally prayed for only a dozen or so before fatigue set in, and his son, "Billy Paul" Branham, would edge up behind him to touch his waist, signaling him to stop. But before sitting down, he would encourage those in the audience to receive healing right where they were. (A personal word here: One night in the Chicago Coliseum on South Wabash Avenue, he pointed out my father some fifteen rows back, identified his serious ulcer condition, and said he would be well. Our whole family broke into tears—only to rejoice in coming months as the healing proved true.)

While his accuracy regarding the sick was remarkable, he could occasionally misread guidance about his own schedule. Gordon Lindsay (see chapter 14) remembers a tense time when he had done all the setup arrangements for a revival series in Minneapolis, only to find the evangelist missing. Where was he? Lindsay finally tracked him down by phone back in Indiana. Branham said he "felt led" not to go after all. Lindsay persuaded him to get in his car regardless and drive through the night to Minneapolis.

On another occasion in South Africa, he wrapped up a successful time in Johannesburg, but then said, while riding south the next day, that the angel had come to him and warned him not to go on to the next city on the preplanned schedule. A tense discussion ensued on the shoulder of the road. In the presence of the whole team, the elderly F. F. Bosworth (in some ways a mentor) dared to rebuke him: "Brother Branham, you're wrong." The evangelist backed down and continued the itinerary.

In matters of doctrine, however, William Branham charted his own course from about 1960 onward, straying outside evangelical guardrails. He had received no theological education, and it showed. He proclaimed the oneness of the Godhead (as opposed to a Trinitarian view), insisting that believers be rebaptized "in the name of the Lord Jesus Christ" if necessary. He embraced annihilationism for the unsaved ("Eternal life was reserved only for God and His children"), opposed all denominations ("a mark of the Beast") and most bizarrely, came to espouse "the serpent's seed," the notion that Eve's fall in the Garden involved more than a piece of fruit; she had in fact been seduced by Lucifer, resulting in the birth of Cain, who became the progenitor of original sin. Consequently, every woman potentially carried "the seed of the Devil," he said.

These aberrations in the later years dimmed Branham's legacy and alienated many of his friends in the ministry. His life came to a tragic end at the age of 56, when he was struck head-on by a drunk driver on a Texas highway; he died on Christmas Eve 1965 in an Amarillo hospital. The faithful prayed fervently for his resurrection all the way up until Easter 1966; when that did not happen, his body was buried the next day.

Perhaps the best way to view the remarkable, if at times eccentric, William Branham is to remember Paul's advice: "Think of what you were when you were called. Not many of you were wise by human standards; not many were influential; not many were of noble birth. But God chose the foolish things of the world to shame the wise; God chose the weak things of the world to shame the strong. God chose the lowly things of this world . . . so that no one may boast before him" (1 Corinthians 1:26–29).

18

Demos Shakarian
(1913–1983)

The Milkman

He clearly was not a preacher, a healing evangelist or even a Christian musician. What he knew best was the dairy business, having learned from his immigrant father. The grandparents and family had fled their native Armenia in 1905 on the basis of a bold prophecy about a coming calamity for Christians in the Muslim-dominated Ottoman Empire (the Armenian genocide that broke loose in 1915, soon after the start of World War I).

Settling in Los Angeles, less than a mile from the fledgling Azusa Street Mission, the Shakarians joined the nearby Armenian Pentecostal Church. It was here that young Demos (born in 1913) gave his life to Christ and, at the age of thirteen, was baptized in the Holy Spirit and also received healing for a hearing difficulty. By then the family had moved a few miles southeast to Downey, California, where land was cheaper, and was busily building what eventually became Reliance Dairy Farms, the nation's largest privately owned herd of milk cows (some three thousand). Demos was taught how to milk them, keep them healthy and sell their daily output at a profit.

Eventually, he and his wife, Rose, wondered what they might do to advance the Lord's work in their area. In 1940, Demos began modestly by setting up tent meetings for itinerant speakers. The first tent seated only three hundred, but in that campaign, 67 were filled with the Spirit. Larger gatherings took place throughout the decade, culminating in a 1948 Hollywood Bowl youth rally that drew 22,000. The bills got paid because Shakarian had spearheaded a fund-raising dinner for a hundred fellow businessmen at Knott's Berry Farm.

The entrepreneur was bothered by something, however, whenever he scanned the typical tent-revival crowd: He saw far more women than men. He began musing to himself and his wife, "Just think how many more businessmen there are in the world than preachers. If businessmen should ever start to spread the gospel . . ." To him, the potential seemed huge. When he helped organize an Oral Roberts campaign in the fall of 1951 (which drew more than two hundred thousand people over sixteen days, with four thousand salvations and thousands of healings), Demos Shakarian took the chance to float an idea with the evangelist: What about some kind of businessmen's fellowship to help spread the Gospel? Roberts gave him warm encouragement.

And so, some two hundred businessmen showed up on a Saturday morning in the upstairs room of the landmark Clifton's Cafeteria in downtown LA. There they organized what became the Full Gospel Business Men's Fellowship International (FGBMFI). It would seek to introduce everyday men to a God strong enough to restore their souls, their relationships, even their bodies—in other words, a *full* gospel. Membership in the group would be open to anyone who was not clergy or female!

Oral Roberts was the main speaker that first morning, closing with a passionate prayer for God to use this group. When he moved on to his next campaign in Fresno, the dairyman followed and gathered another 150 men to the concept. By January, more than a hundred in Phoenix had signed up as well. Incorporation soon followed.

Shakarian's stroke of genius was not to try to duplicate a church service or healing meeting per se. He took his cue more from the noon-luncheon format of such service clubs as Rotary or Kiwanis. Men gathered around hearty food, got to know one another and then listened to a businessman give his personal testimony before returning to the office or other workplace. The microphone was shared widely from Pentecostals to Presbyterians to Methodists to Catholics, thus advancing the wave of the Spirit across all traditions.

The idea caught fire: By 1970, there were three hundred thousand members in seven hundred chapters across America and beyond. Oral Roberts called them "God's Ballroom Saints." FGBMFI "airlifts" took planeloads of Christian businessmen and their wives to Europe, Africa, the Middle East and East Asia to spread the Word.

A monthly digest-size magazine called *Voice* was inaugurated and widely passed around, with life stories of ordinary men and their encounters with an extraordinary God. In 1978, the annual convention drew a peak attendance of 25,000. Every year at the FGBMFI board meeting, Demos Shakarian would resign his position as president and step out into the hall; the board would promptly vote him back in for another year. He never saw himself as more than what 1 Corinthians 12, in its list of spiritual giftings from apostle on down, termed a "helper" in the Body of Christ (see verse 28).

By 1986, the Full Gospel Business Men's ranks had swelled to seven hundred thousand regular attenders in three thousand chapters (1,715 in the United States) across 95 countries, including such hard places as the Soviet Union, Czechoslovakia and Saudi Arabia. The noted authors John and Elizabeth Sherrill wrote a book about the movement entitled *The Happiest People on Earth*. No one could have been happier with the flood of Spirit-energized faith among men than the California milkman Demos Shakarian.

19

Derek Prince
(1915–2003)

Intelligent, Sincere—and Fallible

Whatever stereotype one may hold about Pentecostal/charismatic leaders (flamboyant, emotional, provincial, spell-binding), Derek Prince doesn't fit. Born in Bangalore, India, to British parents, he received a stellar English education back in the UK, first at the elite, boys-only boarding school Eton, then at King's College, Cambridge, where he secured a fellowship in ancient and modern philosophy. He wasn't devout ("Religion doesn't do much for me," he said)—but when packing up for military training in the early days of World War II, he added a Bible out of mild curiosity for what philosophical material it might contain.

During off-duty times, he began reading it. He got about halfway through the Old Testament when, late one night, a dramatic encounter with Jesus Christ took him by surprise. Less than two weeks later, he found himself praying not in English but in something that sounded like Chinese. Throughout the war, while serving as a medic, he continued to grow in spiritual understanding.

At war's end, he was discharged from the British Medical Corps during a posting in Jerusalem. There he, now thirty years old, had happened to meet a mid-forties Danish woman, Lydia Christiansen, who ran an orphanage for girls. In time they were married, and overnight, Prince became the father of eight daughters she had adopted: six Jewish, one Palestinian and one English.

The 1948 Arab-Israeli War chased the family out of the Holy Land; upon returning to London, he established and led a Pentecostal church for the next eight years. After that, the couple moved to a third continent—Africa, where he became the principal of a Kenyan teacher training college. They also adopted another daughter locally during this season.

Only in 1962, when Derek Prince was in his late forties, did he and his family set foot in North America, first in Canada. Then while pastoring in nearby Seattle, he experienced his first face-off with a demonic outburst during a Sunday service and learned how to overcome it—a subject on which he would speak and write extensively later. His speaking style was always serious and straightforward, without flair or cleverness. He used few illustrations as he expounded the Scriptures. At one point, even evangelist Billy Graham called him "my favorite Bible teacher."

His books carried such mainstream titles as *Praying for the Government* and *Shaping History through Prayer and Fasting* and *Faith to Live By*. He especially championed what he viewed as God's plan for the modern state of Israel.

But his name is most connected to the role he played in the controversial "shepherding/discipleship movement" that swept the charismatic landscape during the 1970s and '80s. After moving to south Florida, he and four like-minded Bible teachers (Bob Mumford, Don Basham, Charles Simpson, Ern Baxter) became known as "the Fort Lauderdale Five" through their abundant speaking engagements, books, audiocassettes and articles in their widely circulated magazine called *New Wine*.

In fairness, it must be stated that their quest was not for personal power. They sincerely wanted to address the surging individualism of Spirit-filled believers who were leaving their traditional churches and "flying solo" thereafter, without seasoned guidance. Derek Prince and his associates justifiably began lifting up such admonitions as Hebrews 13:17 ("Obey them that have the rule over you, and submit yourselves: for they watch for your souls, as they that must give account, that they may do it with joy, and not with grief: for that is unprofitable for you" [KJV]) and 1 Corinthians 16:15–16 regarding church leaders ("I urge you, brothers and sisters, to submit to such people and to everyone who joins in the work and labors at it"), among others. After all, hadn't the Catholic church benefited for centuries from the work of godly "spiritual directors"?

If the rising charismatic movement was, to use Jamie Buckingham's colorful phrase, "a balloon with no tether cord," the Fort Lauderdale Five urged the enthusiastic masses to find a shepherd, a "personal pastor" to help them stay on a good path. Those individuals needed to be "under spiritual authority" themselves, of course. Soon these "covenant relationships" began to look more and more like a pyramid scheme, crowned at the top with the Fort Lauderdale Five.

Alarm bells began ringing as early as 1974, when respected Foursquare pastor/author Jack Hayford spoke privately with Bob Mumford. By the next year, Pat Robertson of the Christian Broadcasting Network (CBN) directed his staff not to bring any "shepherding" proponents onto the popular *700 Club* telecast and to erase any such recordings from CBN archives. Demos Shakarian likewise banned Prince and the others from all Full Gospel Business Men's Fellowship events. When Kathryn Kuhlman learned that she would have to share the stage with Mumford at the Second World Conference on the Holy Spirit in Jerusalem, she said she would not come. Mumford quietly backed out.

Why such strong disapprovals? Stories had begun showing up of "shepherds," many of them young, dominating the lives of their "sheep," requiring to receive their tithes, even in some extreme cases dictating which jobs they should take and who might be a suitable person to date or marry. The original call to personal responsibility was mutating into authoritarianism. Three different summit meetings between the Fort Lauderdale Five and their critics were held between August 1975 and March 1976, with little resolution.

Prince's paperback *Discipleship, Shepherding, and Commitment* tried to re-anchor the movement on biblical ground, but the wave was already in motion. At the massive 1977 Kansas City Conference on charismatic renewal in the churches, the shepherding track drew more than nine thousand attenders, second only to the Catholic track with 25,000.

By the early 1980s, however, the movement's head of steam was starting to dissipate as tensions bubbled up in churches and even among the leaders. Derek Prince was the first of the Five to quietly withdraw, admitting "we were guilty of the Galatian error: having begun in the Spirit, we quickly degenerated into the flesh"[1] (see Galatians 3:3). A few more years passed; finally, in November 1988, Bob Mumford penned (with Jack Hayford's encouragement) a seven-paragraph "Formal Repentance Statement to the Body of Christ." Hayford read it aloud to a pastors' conference at his Church on the Way one evening, receiving "general murmurs of agreement" when he finished. The next night in Ridgecrest, North Carolina, Mumford himself—visibly shaken—read it at a major Bible conference.

The scheduled speaker that night was to be none other than Derek Prince. As the crowd of 3,500 politely applauded Mumford's confession, the tall, angular Englishman came to the podium. He followed with his own word of explanation: "I never was involved in asking people to submit to me—I tend to let people go their own way. But I don't believe it was ever God's intent to start a movement. All of us have to share the responsibility . . . of failing God and failing the body of Christ."[2]

Speaking personally, he continued, "I felt God had put us [the Five] together. [But] I allowed loyalty to my fellow ministers to supersede my loyalty to God."[3]

Derek Prince lived another fifteen years, continuing to speak and travel widely. At the age of eighty, he gave a series of forthright talks on the shepherding era to his staff, which were collected into a book entitled *Protection from Deception*. It evidenced regret and chagrin at what he and the others had engendered, urging readers to "prove all things; hold fast that which is good" (1 Thessalonians 5:20–21 KJV).

When he died in his sleep (back in Jerusalem) at the age of 88, his radio broadcasts were still being heard around the globe, not only in English but also translated into Arabic, Chinese, Croatian, Malagasy, Mongolian, Russian, Samoan, Spanish and Tongan. CBN, his onetime critic, posted a gracious tribute on its website that summarized him well: "Derek Prince—father, friend and teacher to the nations."

20

Dennis & Rita Bennett
(1917–1991)/(1934–)

The Reluctant Rector

Father Dennis Bennett had ample reason to be pleased with what St. Mark's Episcopal Church, in the wealthy Los Angeles suburb of Van Nuys, had become during his nearly seven years as rector. A struggling congregation had gotten onto its feet and now numbered 2,600 members. His ministerial staff included four associate priests.

Still, Bennett was not entirely satisfied with his own spiritual state. His solid education (University of Chicago followed by Chicago Theological Seminary) had filled his head but somehow left his heart lukewarm. He longed to regain the passion he had known following his conversion experience back at age eleven.

A fellow priest called him one day and mentioned a couple of parishioners who had quite suddenly become energized in their faith and service to God. They talked about something called the "baptism in the Holy Spirit." Bennett was curious enough to go to a prayer meeting in this colleague's church . . . which led to a Saturday morning meeting of just four people in a private home. In his inaugural book, he tells about feeling self-conscious, even awkward:

> "What do I do?" I asked them again.
> "Ask Jesus to baptize you in the Holy Spirit," said John. "We'll pray with you, and you just pray and praise the Lord."
> I said: "Now remember, I want this nearness of God you have, that's all; I'm not interested in speaking with tongues!"
> "Well," they said, "all we can tell you about that is that it came with the package!"
> John came across the room and laid his hands first on my head, and then on my friend's. He began to pray, very quietly, and I recognized . . . he was speaking in a language that I did not understand, and speaking it very fluently. He wasn't a bit "worked up" about it, either. Then he prayed in English, asking Jesus to baptize me in the Holy Spirit.
> I began to pray, as he told me, and I prayed very quietly, too. I was not about to get even a little bit excited! I was simply following instructions. I suppose I must have prayed out loud for about twenty minutes . . . and was just about to give up when a very strange thing happened. My tongue tripped, just as it might when you are trying to recite a tongue twister, and I began speaking a new language!
> Right away I recognized several things: first, it wasn't some kind of psychological trick or compulsion. . . . I was allowing these new words to come to my lips and was speaking them out of my own volition . . . and it was rather beautiful. . . .[1]

A new joy and intimacy with God rose up in Dennis Bennett's soul, to the point that he dared not keep quiet about it.

His church members asked him what had happened, and he answered their questions. Over a period of weeks, some seventy people asked to follow in his steps and were similarly blessed, including two of the staff priests. Rumors began to spread, however, and finally the rector felt he should come clean with the entire congregation. On Sunday, April 3, 1960, he mounted the pulpit and spilled the whole story.

The reaction that day was dramatic. Some listeners were intrigued, while others rose up in protest. Comments flew through the air. "We are Episcopalians, not a bunch of wild-eyed hillbillies," one man shouted after mounting a chair like a soapbox. "Throw out the damned tongues-speakers!" another yelled.[2] One associate priest dramatically took off his vestments and said that under the circumstances, he had no choice but to resign.

Newspapers picked up the story, and by the next day the wire services had spread it nationwide. Both *Time* and *Newsweek* soon ran articles. Father Bennett was amazed but also troubled about what he should do, especially after his bishop, Francis Eric Bloy, sent out a pastoral letter banning tongues across the Los Angeles diocese. Bennett wrote to charismatic statesman David du Plessis for advice and received wise counsel not to fight, but rather to ask for reassignment elsewhere (see chapter 13 for the details).

By that summer he was installed in a tiny mission church in Seattle, St. Luke's, that was about to be closed for the third time. The situation was so dire that his message about Holy Spirit empowerment was welcomed—anything to help keep the doors open. People warmed to what he was explaining and sought this new dimension for themselves. Attendance began to grow. Life and energy blossomed. Even the death of Bennett's first wife, Elberta, in 1963 did not quench his spirit or the pursuit of his calling. Over the next decade, St. Luke's became a center of renewal and the largest Episcopal parish across the Northwest.

Bennett married again in 1966, to a counselor and teacher named Rita Reed (sister of Dr. William Standish Reed, initiator of the Christian Medical Foundation). She was, in fact, the speaker at a seminal women's meeting in Seattle the next year that evolved into the Aglow International movement. She also helped her husband craft his story into the bestseller *Nine O'Clock in the Morning.*

In 1971, they collaborated again on a practical guidebook called *The Holy Spirit and You,* which again gave direction to seeking believers. They had a unique way with metaphors to explain the baptism in the Holy Spirit: "It *is* a baptism, meaning a drenching, an overflowing, a saturating of your soul and body with the Holy Spirit. . . . The word 'baptize' in Greek means to completely suffuse—it is used in classical Greek of a sunken, water-logged ship."[3]

In another place, they write:

Imagine an irrigation canal in Southern California or some other area that is normally arid most of the year. The canal is dry and so are the fields around. All the vegetation is dried up and dead. Then the gates from the reservoir are opened, and the canal begins to fill with water.

First of all, the canal itself is refreshed! The cool flow of water carries away debris and slakes the dust. Next, grass and flowers begin to spring up along the banks, and the trees on either side of the canal become fresh and green. But it doesn't stop there; all the way along the canal, farmers open the gates, and the life-giving water pours out into the fields. . . .

So it is with you and me. The reservoir, the well, is in us when we become Christians. Then, when we allow the indwelling living water of the Spirit to flow out into our souls and bodies, *we* are refreshed first. . . . Then the living water begins to pour out to others, and they see the power and love of Jesus in His people. He is now able to use us to refresh the world around us.[4]

The invitations to travel and speak became so numerous that in 1981, Dennis Bennett retired from parish work at St. Luke's to assume a wider impact. His bishop, Robert H. Cochrane, recognized him at that point as a "canon of honor" for his work across the charismatic landscape. He was one of the founders of the Episcopal Charismatic Fellowship (later renamed Episcopal Renewal Ministries), contending that "No one needs to leave the Episcopal Church in order to have the fullness of the Spirit—but it is of greatest importance that the Spirit be allowed to work freely in the Episcopal Church."[5]

Ever since Dennis's death in 1991, Rita Bennett has continued to write and minister, especially in the areas of inner healing and emotional freedom.[6] Together, their mature influence has been invaluable not only for Episcopalians, but also across the denominational spectrum worldwide.

21

Kenneth E. Hagin
(1917–2003)

Speak It, Believe It, Receive It

Whenever two or three charismatics are gathered together, there will be four or more opinions about Kenneth Hagin, father of the "Word of Faith" (or "Positive Confession") movement. To some, the teachings of the mild-mannered, grandfatherly Texan have opened the gates to a fuller life of spiritual, physical and material abundance. To others, his doctrine is seriously flawed. And that's just for starters.

Born and raised among Southern Baptists, Hagin's interest in health was not just theoretical; he had a congenital heart malformation plus a blood disease that meant a childhood of sickness. At the age of fifteen, he committed his life to Christ, and a year later, though bedridden, was dramatically healed after focusing on Mark 11:23–24—"For verily I say unto you,

That whosoever shall say unto this mountain, Be thou removed, and be thou cast into the sea; and shall not doubt in his heart, but shall believe that those things which he saith shall come to pass; he shall have whatsoever he saith. Therefore I say unto you, What things soever ye desire, when ye pray, believe that ye receive them, and ye shall have them" (KJV). In years to come, he would quote these verses repeatedly.

He founded a nondenominational church before his twentieth birthday, and after learning about Spirit baptism at a Pentecostal tent meeting, pastored Assemblies of God congregations throughout the 1940s. In 1949, he began to travel as a Bible teacher and evangelist, eventually headquartering in Garland, Texas, for a number of years before relocating to Tulsa in 1966. By then he had a daily radio program called "Faith Seminar of the Air" and was articulating his signature message: that God would respond to what believers declared in faith, resulting in all manner of good and godly things. After all, didn't the Bible say, "Death and life are in the power of the tongue: and they that love it shall eat the fruit thereof" (Proverbs 18:21 KJV)? Hadn't God instructed Moses and Aaron, "Say unto them, As truly as I live, saith the LORD, as ye have spoken in mine ears, so will I do to you" (Numbers 14:28 KJV)?

And hadn't the apostle John clearly written, "Beloved, I wish above all things that thou mayest prosper and be in health, even as thy soul prospereth" (3 John 2 KJV)?

Over Kenneth Hagin's long life, he would pen and self-publish more than a hundred brief books with such titles as *How to Write Your Own Ticket with God* and *How God Taught Me about Prosperity*. His most popular work was *The Believer's Authority* (1985), which has sold more than a million copies; the back cover declares:

Do we have authority that we don't know about—that we haven't discovered—that we're not using?

. . . A few of us have barely gotten to the edge of that authority, but before Jesus comes again, there's going to be a whole company of believers who will rise up and with the authority that is theirs . . . they will do the work that God intended they should do.

Today, that "whole company" includes some 26,000 graduates of Rhema Bible Training College in Broken Arrow, Oklahoma (greater Tulsa), plus another sixty thousand from parallel schools on 253 campuses in 51 countries. Thousands come each July to the weeklong Rhema Camp meeting; many more watch the weekly *Rhema Praise* TV program and share videos with one another. Nearly every city in America has one or more local churches in the Word of Faith vein.

Younger speakers have looked to "Dad" Hagin as a mentor and followed his lead: Kenneth and Gloria Copeland, Joyce Meyer, Creflo Dollar, Frederick K. C. Price, to name just a few—not to mention his own son and daughter-in-law, Kenneth W. and Lynette Hagin, who now lead the Rhema ministries.

As is well known, however, serious questions have been raised about the Positive Confession teaching, particularly its focus on health and prosperity. Scholars have criticized the cherry-picking of Scripture bits—for example, "The word is nigh thee, even in thy mouth, and in thy heart: that is, the word of faith, which we preach" (Romans 10:08 KJV). They say the popular 3 John 2 verse is nothing more than a simple greeting along the lines of "I hope you're doing well these days." One of the first theologians to speak up was Charles Farah Jr., of nearby Oral Roberts University, who in 1979 wrote *From the Pinnacle of the Temple,* cautioning against human presumption that

God would do whatever we say. An ORU graduate named D. R. McConnell produced a substantive challenge in his book *A Different Gospel* (1988).

By then, respected New Testament scholar and Bible translator Gordon D. Fee (whose background, like Hagin's, was Assemblies of God) wrote a series of articles entitled "The Disease of the Health & Wealth Gospels," calling readers to remember the Bible's predisposition toward the poor and humble. In one conclusion, Fee wrote: "Any 'Gospel' that will not 'sell' as well among believers in Ouagadougou, Upper Volta or Dacca, Bangladesh . . . as in Orange County, California, or Tulsa County, Oklahoma, is *not* the Gospel of our Lord Jesus Christ."[1]

But to be fair in assessing the Kenneth Hagin teaching (often mocked as "name it and claim it" or even more crassly as "blab it and grab it"), one must not pass over the last book he wrote, at the age of 83, entitled *The Midas Touch—A Balanced Approach to Biblical Prosperity*. In his introduction, he admitted:

During my more than sixty-five years of ministry, I have . . . observed many teachings and practices that have both helped and hindered the Body of Christ. . . .

It has been my experience that with virtually every biblical subject, there is a main road of truth with a ditch of error on either side of the road. The Church has not always been a very good driver, often having great difficulty staying in the middle of the road. . . .

The topic of money and prosperity is no exception. There are those in the ditch on one side of the road who teach that Jesus lived in abject poverty, that money is evil, and that biblical prosperity has nothing at all to do with material things. And in the other ditch, there are people who are preaching that getting rich is the main focus of faith, that God's main concern is your material well-being, and that money is the true measure of spirituality. Where is the truth? It's found far away from both extremes, on much higher ground.[2]

Hagin then went on to censure . . .

- Those who "try to make the offering plate some kind of heavenly vending machine. . . . There is no spiritual formula to sow a Ford and reap a Mercedes."
- Those who ask audiences to "name your seed" (a specific amount of money they will give in order to get a larger return blessing). He said this "corrupts the very attitude of our giving nature."
- Similarly, he said the notion of "a hundredfold return" was not biblical. He did the math and concluded that if this were true, "we would have Christians walking around with not billions or trillions of dollars, but quadrillions of dollars!"
- Those who preached "supernatural debt cancellation" via giving were told, "There is not one bit of Scripture I know about that validates such a practice. I'm afraid it is simply a scheme to raise money for the preacher."
- He especially tackled one radio preacher who told listeners he would take their prayer requests to Jesus at "'the empty tomb in Jerusalem and pray over them there'—if donors included a special love gift. What that radio preacher really wanted was more people to send in offerings."

Kenneth E. Hagin sincerely wanted Christians to be able to live more abundant lives on every level. And for that—however imperfectly stated—who can fault him?

22

Harald Bredesen
(1918–2006)

The Happy Envoy

You may not recognize the name *Harald Bredesen*, unless you have read the 1964 classic (2.5 million copies sold) *They Speak with Other Tongues*. Chapter 2, entitled "Harald's Strange Story," tells how award-winning Episcopal author/researcher John L. Sherrill took him to lunch upon recommendation of a fellow *Guideposts* magazine editor.

Bredesen, pastor of the First Reformed Church in the New York City suburb of Mount Vernon, showed up with "a clerical collar, a bald spot and an excitement that was contagious. . . . There, in a setting of coffee cups and sugar shakers, he told me a story that seemed to come from a different world."[1]

He had become so dissatisfied with the gap between first-century Christianity and the modern version that he had gone off to a mountain cabin for a multiday spiritual retreat. There at last one morning, as he stood outside gazing at the Alleghenies, he paused in his praying . . . and then came an outpouring of words he did not recognize. "It was as though I was listening to a foreign language," the minister told Sherrill, "except that it was coming out of my own mouth."

> Amazed, curious, and a bit frightened, Bredesen ran down the mountain, still talking aloud in this tongue. He came to the edge of a small community. On the stoop of a cabin sat an old man. Bredesen continued to speak in the tongue which was coming so easily and naturally from his lips. The man answered, talking rapidly in a language which Bredesen did not know. When it became obvious that they were not communicating, the old man spoke in English.
>
> "How can you speak Polish but not understand it?" the man asked.
>
> "*I* was speaking in Polish?"
>
> The man laughed, thinking that Bredesen was joking. "Of course it was Polish," he said.
>
> But Bredesen wasn't joking. As far as he could recall he had never before heard the language.[2]

This certainly was not anything like what young Harald had seen or heard growing up in the Minnesota church his Norwegian father pastored. When he studied for the ministry at Luther College (Decorah, Iowa), no one had uttered a word about such goings-on. He was in uncharted territory for sure.

Nevertheless, from that day in the mountains, Bredesen would spend the rest of his life—close to fifty years—explaining the baptism in the Holy Spirit and the vitality it spawns. He would address the curious and the critical alike, starting with his own congregation. First Reformed began a series of late-Sunday-afternoon prayer meetings, in the old stone sanctuary, simply called "Vespers" to welcome spiritual gifts; starting at 4:00 p.m., they would run as late as 6 or 7. Led by Bredesen and his young seminary intern, Pat Robertson (of future CBN fame), people worshiped freely and waited expectantly for the Spirit's touch.

Visitors started showing up: *New York Times* assistant national editor Bob Slosser for one, who after being Spirit-filled went on to write books with charismatic notables David du Plessis and Everett (Terry) Fullam; John Sherrill and his writer wife, Elizabeth; reporters from *Time* and the Associated Press; a film crew from Walter Cronkite's *CBS Evening News*.

Soon the clergyman was invited to broaden his impact at nearby Ivy League schools such as Harvard, Princeton and Yale, where a remarkable awakening took place, with many students speaking in tongues (the press dubbed them "glossoyalies"). By the time he had taken the stage as far away as the University of Chicago and at Stanford on the West Coast, the *Saturday Evening Post* crowned him "charismatic envoy to the campuses."

Being based in the New York City area made it convenient to meet such people as the young minister to gang members David Wilkerson and connect him with John Sherrill; together they wrote *The Cross and the Switchblade*. Another younger personality greatly influenced by Bredesen and his wife, Genevieve, was the pop singer Pat Boone. In one book introduction, Boone wrote, "Abraham . . . Moses . . . Gideon . . . Elijah . . . I think I've known a man like these. His name is Harald Bredesen. Miracles trail him wherever he goes."

All of these found that his heart for God was infectious, as they watched him walking around praising aloud and often venturing into tongues. He was known to follow the Spirit's leading in unpredictable ways, sometimes showing up unannounced to see prominent figures. He built a warm friendship with Egyptian president Anwar Sadat, for example, eventually honoring him with a new prize he had invented called "Prince of Peace." (Other recipients in later years: Mother Teresa, King Hussein of Jordan and Billy Graham.) Sadat called it "the high point of my entire life, more important to me even than the Nobel Peace Prize. That was in the political arena. This was spiritual."

How do we summarize the life and ministry of Harald Bredesen? He was, apparently, the first ordained minister from a mainline denomination to receive the baptism in the Holy Spirit, speak about it openly and not get forced out. His sunny disposition and his energetic bounce were apparently too winsome to oppose. At the same time, the Lord's hand of blessing on his life was too obvious to dismiss.

23

Oral Roberts
(1918–2009)

Rise Up

The first-grade teacher smiled as she welcomed her young students for the opening day of school. "We're going to start by having each of you tell me your name," she said in a pleasant voice. All proceeded smoothly until she came to one dark-haired boy, whose lips moved and then began to quiver. Seconds of silence passed awkwardly.

Finally, he stuttered, "O . . . Or . . . Or . . . Oral . . . R-r-roberts." Several classmates snickered.

From that day forward, the teasing persisted on the playground, in the hall, on the way home from school. Even at family gatherings, one uncle laughed heartily at the boy's struggle to frame syllables. Who had ever thought to name this kid *Oral*, of all things?!

He might not have been able to speak fluently, but as he grew tall, he could at least put a basketball in the hoop. During his high school years, he tried to ignore the persistent cough that sometimes brought up dark bits of phlegm. Then, on a winter night in early 1935, just as he was driving for the basket to help his team win the Southern Oklahoma District Championship, he suddenly collapsed onto the floor, gasping for breath, with blood running out of his mouth. His coach picked him up, wrapped him in his overcoat and drove him home.

"Lying in the back seat of Mr. Hamilton's car I felt my life shattered," he later wrote. "I wanted to die: I prayed to die. But I knew that the prayers of my godly parents were catching up to me."[1]

Lying in bed helpless for weeks, visiting doctors concurred that the young man had been stricken with tuberculosis. His coughing became so violent that, at one point, the blood-spattered wallpaper had to be replaced. His father, a minister in the Pentecostal Holiness Church, sought to get his son into a sanitarium one hundred miles east, but there was no open bed.

And then that summer, Oral's older brother heard about a tent revival in Ada, Oklahoma, that including praying for the sick. He borrowed a car to take him and their parents there. With his father and mother holding up their feeble son, the evangelist approached, touched Oral's head and prayed a short but forceful prayer: "Thou foul disease, I command you in the name of Jesus of Nazareth to leave this body!"

In the flash of a second, faith leaped out of my heart as I let it go to God. It seemed all the pent-up force of my soul was released in that indescribable moment of believing. A blinding flash of light engulfed me and . . . I felt light as a feather. . . .

131

The healing power [surged] through every fiber again and again until I shouted at the top of my voice, "I'm healed! I'm healed!"[2]

Stuttering vanished as well that night. Within months, the young man had both the lung strength and the fluency to become the junior preacher in his father's evangelistic campaigns. By the time he neared the age of 21, he married Evelyn, and for the next decade they either pastored small Pentecostal Holiness churches or led revival meetings. Along the way, he took classes at two different Christian colleges, while the first of the couple's eventual four children was born.

It was in late 1946 that Oral Roberts, now 28 years old, was called to pray for a deacon whose foot had been crushed by a heavy motor. Within seconds, the man was restored and pain-free. By the next year, Roberts decided to resign his pastorate and venture out into a full-time healing ministry. One night while praying for a small boy who was deaf in one ear, he heard God's voice say, "Son, you have been faithful up to this hour, and now you will feel My presence in your right hand." Immediately his right hand grew warm, while nothing happened in his left. This became a sign for the rest of his life whenever he prayed for the sick.

Throughout the 1950s and beyond, the crusades of Oral Roberts led the surge of a healing phenomenon across the nation and beyond. He set up his headquarters in Tulsa. His largest "tent cathedral" seated crowds of more than 12,500. He began a monthly magazine, *Healing Waters* (later renamed *Abundant Life*), which reached a circulation of one million. In 1955, he began a weekly telecast of his meetings that brought the reality of healing into America's living rooms. It rose to the number-one slot in syndicated religious programs for almost thirty years, airing on 135 of the nation's 500 TV stations. His mailing list quickly doubled.

The elites complained, of course. "If Brother Roberts wishes to exploit hysteria and ignorance by putting up his hands and yelling 'Heal,'" wrote a *New York Times* TV and radio critic, "that is his affair, but it hardly seems within the public interest . . . for the TV industry to go along with him."[3] The National Council of Churches voiced its displeasure as well, lobbying Congress to ban *all* religious programs. A 1956 campaign in Australia had to be cut short due to widespread pushback from secular newspapers as well as Christian opponents.

Oral Roberts declined to defend himself; he was too busy. In more than three hundred major crusades between 1947 and 1968, he is estimated to have personally laid hands on as many as two million people seeking healing (including this author). His monthly column ran in 674 newspapers. In 1966, evangelist Billy Graham invited him to the Berlin Congress on World Evangelism, and also agreed to speak the next year at the formal dedication of Tulsa's new Oral Roberts University. This, said Roberts, would be a first-class institution to train graduates "to go where His light is dim, where His voice is heard small, and His healing power is not known." The ultramodern architecture of the 323-acre campus, with its two-hundred-foot steel and glass Prayer Tower, became a major tourist attraction. The ORU Titans basketball team quickly began making waves as well, winning selection into the March Madness playoffs repeatedly, while President Roberts cheered from the sidelines.

Innovation did not scare him at all. He shut down his popular TV program in 1968 so he could retool it the next year into a studio-based variety show format. Interview guests ran the gamut from Roy Rogers to Mahalia Jackson; music poured forth from ORU's World Action Singers troupe (including the future Kathie Lee Gifford), coached by renowned songwriter/ arranger Ralph Carmichael. And on each segment, Oral Roberts would face the camera and implore his viewers to "expect a miracle!"

More than a few traditional supporters were jostled about that same time when he opted to switch his ordination from Pentecostal Holiness to Methodist. *What could he be thinking?* many wondered. The backstory was that his grandfather, "Judge" Amos Roberts, had been a Methodist steward, and now Oral and his wife had found a warm welcome at Tulsa's Boston Avenue Methodist Church. The new affiliation would fit well with his broader acceptance across denominational lines. Said the bishop, "We need you, but we need the Holy Spirit more . . . we've got to have the Holy Spirit in the Methodist Church." (Roberts did clarify, however, that ORU would remain independent.)

Not every venture blossomed under his entrepreneurial touch. The City of Faith Medical and Research Center he opened in 1981 next to the ORU campus with an impressive sixty-story tower was meant to merge medicine and prayer in the healing process. Roberts said he was sure God had commissioned this through a vision of a nine-hundred-foot-tall Jesus, telling him to find a cure for cancer. However, the costs were astronomical, forcing the center's closure eight years later. The property had to be sold to business interests, who renamed it CityPlex Towers.

About the same time, Roberts set out to raise eight million dollars for sending missionary healing teams, stating in an appeal letter: "I desperately need you to come into agreement with me. . . . God said, 'I want you to use the ORU medical school to put My medical presence in the earth. I want you to get this going in one year, or I will call you home!'" Again, was he serious? Had God actually put him on a twelve-month countdown to live? Or was this a case of spiritual blackmail? The religious world was abuzz.

Historian David Harrell, his biographer, told *Christianity Today*, "Some are saying Oral is a swindler. It's not that simple. I firmly believe he thinks he heard from God. I'm sure he had people around him who advised against going public with this because of the ramifications. . . . The best indication of Oral's sincerity is his lack of pragmatism."[4]

Whatever the truth, the money did come in just in time, and Oral Roberts went on to live another 22 years. He relinquished his ORU leadership to his son Richard in 1993, with the university deeply in debt. A seventy-million-dollar bailout came in 2007 from Hobby Lobby retail magnate David Green and his family, provided Richard resign and better financial controls be instituted. The school continues today on more solid ground.

As for the semi-retired Oral Roberts, he died peacefully in late 2009 at the age of 91 from pneumonia. He will be forever remembered as the one who rose up from small-town Oklahoma obscurity to assure the world that "God is a good God!" (another of his signature phrases) and is fully willing to address His people's pain with miracle power.

24

Tommy Tyson
(1922–2002)

The Methodist Who Stayed

The young pastor was nervous about meeting with his bishop. He had recently been baptized in the Holy Spirit through the influence of a scholarly but deeply spiritual acquaintance, and when he told the parishioners of Bethany Methodist Church (Durham, North Carolina) what had happened to him, they were not entirely positive. Tommy Tyson—son of a Methodist minister and brother of five more Methodist ministers—felt he should come clean with his superior.

He described the situation to Bishop Paul Garber and stated, "If no more than I have now is causing this kind of a reaction, there's no telling what will happen if the Lord really gets hold of me." Maybe, he speculated, he should just go back to being a layman. "I am already packed," he said.

The bishop shook his head. "Now, you just go back and unpack that bag," the older man replied. "You're not going anyplace. We need you. We want you. But you need us, too." Both men had read enough Methodist history to know that faith was more than head knowledge and tradition. Hadn't the eighteenth-century founder, John Wesley, written in his journal about prayer meetings where "the power of God came mightily upon us, insomuch that many cried out for exceeding joy, and many fell to the ground"[1]?

By two years later (1954), Tommy Tyson had completed a master of divinity degree at nearby Duke University and been formally appointed as a conference evangelist. No doubt his hearty laugh and folksy manner helped win over his ministry colleagues as he began to travel and speak at spiritual retreats. (Some people in later years said he even reminded them of the comedian Jonathan Winters.) But there was a serious side to Tyson, as well; he drew much from Quaker devotional classics to teach about "listening prayer."

An international prayer movement called Camps Farthest Out invited him often to lead events. It was at one of these, in 1963, that he met healing exponent Oral Roberts. The two struck up a friendship. A couple of years later, Roberts (soon to become a Methodist himself; see chapter 23) asked Tyson to become the inaugural chaplain at the new university he was opening in Tulsa. Once again, the bishop approved, and so starting in 1965, Tyson guided the spiritual formation of hundreds of young students.

In the words of one young man posted on a tribute website, "His broad smile and bellowing laugh would melt ice in Alaska. He was disarmingly warm and gracious to everyone, then become a lion in the pulpit, challenging young Christians to a deeper relationship with Christ. . . . I had the honor of seeing

Tommy up close his last year at ORU. He was a great man of faith and a spiritual father to so many."[2]

In 1968, Tyson and his wife, Frances, returned to their home roots in North Carolina. There they established a Christian getaway called Aquaduct Conference Center, where seeking souls could meet with God. When not ministering there, Tyson resumed his travels, leading spiritual healing conferences alongside everyone from medical doctors to Catholic clergy. Even the Methodist bishop of Cuba asked him to come there for ministry, but dictator Fidel Castro said no. His reason, he said, was that Tyson would bring the Holy Spirit to that island nation, and he did not want it.

In 1983, the National Association of United Methodist Evangelists (NAUME) gave Tyson its distinguished "Philip Award" in recognition of his influence across the denomination and beyond. He left his mark on such well-known pilgrims as Ruth Carter Stapleton (evangelist and sister of President Jimmy Carter), Fr. Francis and Judith MacNutt, and author Madeleine L'Engle.

So wide was his reach that, upon his death at the age of eighty, United Methodist theologian William Cannon said, "Tommy was better known in Rome than in Raleigh." His winsome manner and gentle spirit assured thousands of charismatics that their walk in Spirit fullness did not need to push them away from their ecclesiastical heritage.

25

T. L. & Daisy Osborn
(1923–2013)/(1924–1995)

"Prove It"

The rookie missionary couple got plenty of surprises when they landed in Lucknow, India, in 1945. Along with the language and food differences, they had not expected the Muslims they met to be so gracious. In the open-air marketplace, traders would greet them with "Good morning! Praise God today!" Conversation soon showed that they, too, claimed allegiance to the God of Abraham, Isaac and Jacob.

"So we began to tell them about Jesus," the Osborns recounted years later on a Christian television show. "Yes, they thought He was a wonderful man! His teachings were even in their Qur'an, they said. We told about the miracles of Jesus. Oh yes, they knew He had been a healer."

What next?

The smiles faded "when I came to 'He died for our sins.' The reaction was *no, no, no.* 'God raised him from the dead on the third day . . .' *no, no, no.* My insistence that Jesus was alive hit a brick wall."

The Muslim response to these Gospel truths was, *Prove it, and we'll believe it!* The couple opened their Bibles to show the reality of a living Christ—which only led to debates with the Qur'an, an equally holy book in their minds. The dialogue soon deadlocked.

In the evenings, T. L. (Tommy Lee) and Daisy looked at one another and said, "We don't have any proof, do we? We're just embarrassing God and the Christian faith. We need to get out of here." They retreated to America after just ten months, perplexed and discouraged.

They took up the pastorate of a small church forty miles southwest of Portland, Oregon, and earnestly sought for new understanding. They prayed, searched the Scriptures, read books and tried unsuccessfully to contact people with miracle ministries. What about Aimee Semple McPherson? Sadly, she had passed away by then. So had Smith Wigglesworth, Charles S. Price and other notables. All the giants of faith seemed out of reach. Was there no *current* demonstration of the power of God?

In November 1947, William Branham arrived to hold meetings in the Portland Civic Auditorium. Daisy went one night and came home telling her husband, "You have to come see this! He's a humble man, he doesn't shout or scare anybody—he just believes Jesus is 'the same yesterday, today and forever.' And miracles start happening!"

T. L. attended with his wife and began weeping as he saw visible healings take place. He watched the evangelist engage a young girl who was both deaf and mute. He uttered a simple statement of faith, then snapped his fingers—and she could suddenly hear as well as speak. In that moment, T. L. said, "There seemed to be a thousand voices speaking to me at once, all in one accord saying over and over, 'You can do that, too.'" The Osborns plunged into extended times of prayer and fasting throughout the winter; they also began praying for the sick in their church and seeing results. One woman on crutches after a bad car accident was suddenly able to walk normally around the room—with her eyes closed. Afterward, she said she had heard a choir of angels singing praises to God.

By spring 1948, the erstwhile missionary couple took their message of God's saving and healing power to Jamaica, where hundreds were converted and many ailments disappeared. Back in the United States, they affiliated with the Voice of Healing network and continued with crusades from Michigan to Pennsylvania to Texas that drew ever larger audiences. T. L.'s message was unwavering, drawn straight from the example of the New Testament era; in a booklet entitled *3 Keys to the Book of Acts*, he laid out his formula:

1. They preached the *Word*.
2. They were filled and anointed with the *Spirit*.
3. They knew the authority of, and used, the *Name*.

The *Word* convicted and convinced.
The *Name* was their credentials and authority.
The *Spirit* confirmed and produced the miracles.[1]

He had no time for a theory of cessationism:

Many voices today would have us believe that when Christ ascended to the Father, miracles ceased. The Book of Acts is proof to the contrary.

141

There are many who would have us believe that when the Apostles died, miracles ceased. This again is not true. Since that day the ministry of every man or woman who has been bold enough in faith to follow the example laid down in the Book of Acts has been confirmed by signs and wonders through the power of the Name of Jesus Christ.

There are many voices which would have us believe that miracles were wrought only to establish the Church. This again is not true. What good is a Church established by miracles, if it ceases to perform miracles today?

The blind are not interested in His power to heal the blind only in Bible days. They need His healing *today*.

Let us never depart from the example of the Book of Acts.[2]

The Osborns carried this strong belief for the next forty years to more than seventy countries and territories: Puerto Rico (eighteen thousand conversions in twelve days, 1950), Cuba (fifty thousand conversions, early 1951), thousands more in Venezuela (where doctors and priests got so many reports of healing that they pressed the police to arrest him for "witchcraft"), Guatemala City (another fifty thousand conversions in the midst of political upheaval), and farther abroad to Kenya, Indonesia, Taiwan, Japan, Holland, Chile and Switzerland. In one 1956 meeting in Thailand, more than one hundred people claimed they saw Jesus walking through the crowd.

The organizing genius for all of these gatherings was Daisy Osborn. She firmly believed that women had more than a sideline role to play in God's work. When she spoke publicly, she brought new insight into Bible passages that had long been used to hold women back. She eventually wrote three books on the subject: *Woman Without Limits*, *The Woman Believer* and *5 Choices for Women Who Win*.

Her husband applauded her, knowing that he alone—or even the two of them—could not accomplish everything God had in mind. They also admitted that one series of mass meetings in a given city would fade away without follow-up nurturing of the new converts. This led them to work hard at training national pastors through what the Osborns called the Association for Native Evangelism. They agreed to provide sound and movie equipment as well as pay a salary for twelve months only, after which the recipient was expected to have raised up a supporting congregation. Some four hundred new churches were planted each year. Their stories were featured every month in a magazine called *Faith Digest,* whose circulation reached 670,000.

For the Osborns, the supernatural was never the goal; it served rather to draw lost humanity all around the world to the divine Son of God. An oft-posted quote from T. L. Osborn says it well: "Speaking in tongues is not enough. If we [are to] turn men from unchristian religions to Christianity, we must produce miracles which convince men that Christ lives and He is real today."

26

John & Elizabeth Sherrill

(1923–2017) / (1928–)

The Scribes

When they met in 1947, somewhere in the mid-Atlantic aboard the original *Queen Elizabeth* ocean liner, waves of romance temporarily jostled their thoughts about upcoming study at the University of Geneva. Scarcely four months later they were married, destined to become perhaps the most noted husband-wife writing duo in Christian publishing.

Neither of them were especially religious at the start. They simply had a gift for finding and telling stories that grabbed attention. In 1951, when John got a quick job interview (in a New York City taxi, no less) with Norman Vincent Peale, founder of *Guideposts* magazine, he admitted he was not much interested in religion. He just wanted to write.

"That's an interesting answer," Peale responded. "You're exactly the kind of person I wanted to reach when I started *Guideposts*, people turned off by religious jargon. We want to provide glimpses of God in everyday life all around us."

John got the job as an associate editor, and a few months later, Elizabeth was hired, as well. They were key players over the coming years in the surge of *Guideposts* up to two million copies a month, the biggest paid-circulation Christian magazine in America. And while drafting great stories, their own spiritual lives came alive once they had to face John's cancer diagnosis in 1959.

Some stories deserved more space than the normal two- or three-page magazine format, and so the Sherrills ventured into book creation. One of the earliest was *The Cross and the Switchblade* (1962) with David Wilkerson, the gutsy young Assemblies of God minister who dared to take the Gospel to street thugs. The story was David's, of course; the scintillating prose came from John and "Tib," as Elizabeth was often called. It quickly became a mega-seller.

Wilkerson's theology connected with something that had happened a couple of years earlier, when Mrs. Peale came breezing into a *Guideposts* editorial meeting late, having just spent time with a fascinating dinner guest named Harald Bredesen (see chapter 22). John relates:

"Have you ever heard the expression, 'speaking in tongues'?" she asked.

Most of us had a vague recollection of the phrase. It came from the Bible, I thought. . . .

"Well, my dinner guest said that he had had this experience himself. Not only he, but some of his friends, too. Norman and I sat spell-bound for two hours while he told us about people all over the country who are having this happen to them. . . . It sounds crazy, doesn't it? But there's something about this man. . . ." She paused. "Well, I for one want to know more about it."[1]

John's interest was mildly piqued. He arranged to meet Bredesen himself, who put him in touch with the eminent Dr. Henry Van Dusen, president of Union Theological Seminary, where John's father had, in fact, taught. Van Dusen told about visiting a Pentecostal church service somewhere in the Caribbean and, though finding it very different, being intrigued. He concluded that day in his office by saying, "I have come to feel that the Pentecostal movement with its emphasis upon the Holy Spirit is more than just another revival. It is a revolution in our day . . . comparable in importance with the establishment of the original Apostolic Church and with the Protestant Reformation."[2]

That was enough to set John Sherrill on a course of researching a possible book. He mapped out Old Testament and New Testament references to the Spirit's activity. He started digging into the history of glossolalia in centuries past. He managed to find a few elderly eyewitnesses from the Azusa Street Revival of 1906. He talked to denominational executives, pro and con. When he sat down with a book publisher to get serious about a contract, he told the acquiring editor named Sam Peters:

"There's one thing we'd better keep straight. . . . You keep saying, 'these tongues of yours.' They're not my tongues, Peters, and won't be either. I'm interested, I'm intrigued, but I'm certainly not buying. I'm an Episcopalian, you know, and I guess we're a pretty stuffy lot."

Peters smiled. "I know. No one's asking you to get involved. Just do a good job reporting. That's all we ask."

"Good," I said. "Then we understand each other. I've always said the best reporter, anyway, is the one who keeps his distance."[3]

John Sherrill kept his distance through multiple visits to Pentecostal prayer meetings. He even invited tongues-speakers to stop by his *Guideposts* office so he could tape-record their utterances and then have them analyzed by professional linguists. He interviewed charismatic leaders such as David du Plessis and Dennis Bennett.

Eventually, in 1964, his book *They Speak with Other Tongues* came out—including a chapter near the end that told about his own baptism in the Holy Spirit at a Full Gospel Business Men's convention in Atlantic City. Only five other people were in the fourth-floor hotel room that afternoon when it happened: a Presbyterian clergy couple, two Episcopalians and a Methodist. After considerable sharing, they encircled him and began to pray in concert, some in English, some in tongues.

> It was almost as if they were forming with their bodies a funnel through which was concentrated the flow of the Spirit that was pulsing through that room. It flowed into me as I sat there, listening to the Spirit-song around me. Now the tongues swelled to a crescendo, musical and lovely. I opened my mouth. . . .
>
> From deep inside me, deeper than I knew voice could go, came a torrent of joyful sound. . . . I prayed on, laughing and free, while the setting sun shone through the window, and the stars came out.[4]

Sherrill's book rocked presumptions all across the Christian world. Its thorough research and measured tone gave pause to many skeptics. It became a major catalyst for increasing openness to the Holy Spirit invasion throughout the 1960s and beyond.

Both John and Elizabeth would go on to pen other gripping stories of God's grace and power in human lives. In 1971, they even started a publishing house with their close friends Leonard and Catherine Marshall LeSourd, called Chosen Books. Their first release was a home run: *The Hiding Place* with World War II survivor Corrie ten Boom. A few years later came Watergate "hatchet man" Charles Colson's dramatic *Born Again*. The brand continues to this day, releasing books on spiritual renewal across all sectors of the body of Christ.

John Sherrill lived to the age of 94—not quite long enough to be honored with Elizabeth by the Evangelical Christian Publishers Association (ECPA) with a lifetime achievement award. "Their contributions . . . as writers, editors and publishers to the world of books, and their impact on the Kingdom of God," said the organization, "cannot be overstated. They wrote thousands of magazine articles; crafted more than thirty books (with sales in excess of sixty million); taught narrative technique to generations of new writers; and . . . gave hope to millions of people. The way they wrote set the gold standard for storytelling today."

Christianity Today put it even more succinctly, calling the Sherrills "the most influential Christian authors you know nothing about."

27

Francis & Judith MacNutt

(1925–2020)/(1948–)

Divine Radiology

If you were Roman Catholic in the 1970s (like one-fourth of all Americans), and you had a physical problem that doctors could not seem to solve, where would you have turned? Would you have ventured to one of those Protestant tent meetings or boisterous arenas, with their lively singing and exuberant hand-raising? Maybe not. Should you ask your priest to recite Pope Pius XII's "Consecration of the Sick to Mary" on your behalf? Should you attempt an expensive pilgrimage to the grotto of Lourdes, in France, or Fátima in Portugal? What else could you do?

Hopefully, someone would have told you about an articulate, handsome, six-foot-four-inch Dominican friar in St. Louis named Francis MacNutt. His credentials were impeccable: a bachelor's degree from Harvard, a master's degree from Catholic University of America (Washington, DC) and a PhD from the Dominicans' Aquinas Institute of Theology. A noteworthy preacher, he had served as president of the Catholic Homiletic Society; he was the founding editor of its magazine.

And he openly prayed for the sick.

"We are now seeing a return of the direct experience of God's healing power," he wrote in his 1974 book *Healing* (published by no less than Ave Maria Press) "in such striking ways that . . . [it] is leading us again to a more lively awareness of what Jesus did in his healing ministry. . . . Everywhere I travel I discover that people are experiencing firsthand the healing power of God. The climate is changing."[1] (The book ended up selling a million copies.)

How had this come about? Back in 1967, MacNutt had been invited to a weeklong retreat where he met both Agnes Sanford (Episcopalian) and Tommy Tyson (Methodist). He ended up asking them to pray for him to be baptized in the Holy Spirit. Before week's end, Agnes Sanford prophesied that he would be used to bring healing prayer back into the Catholic Church. He knew well that Jesus and the early apostles had healed the sick in their day. He began praying for the same thing now— and saw people set free of everything from asthma to allergies, heart disease to high blood pressure, torn arches to cancer. Even mental disorders and demonic liaisons were broken.

He did not mount mass crusades in stadiums or launch a TV program. When he prayed for individuals, he was quiet and unhurried; at the end of a meeting, he would personally lay hands on no more than ten or fifteen people, one by one. "Healing takes time," he said. "I just listen, love and pray."

In fact, he wrote in his second book, *The Power to Heal*, that "for many people—probably for most people—a single prayer for healing is not sufficient." Referencing how Jesus prayed twice for a blind man (Mark 8:22–26), MacNutt continued, "If even Jesus had to pray for a person twice, we can certainly expect to have to pray three times or more for the chronic sufferers who come to us for help. This much has become abundantly clear: prayer for healing *is often a process. It requires time*" (italics his).[2] He wrote at length about what he (and others) called "soaking prayer," calling it a form of "God's radiation treatment."

> Just as we know that a single visit of a cancer patient to the hospital to get cobalt radiation treatment is not likely to kill all the cancer cells, so we should not be surprised that it may take more than one session of prayer to cure a chronic illness. . . . And by time to pray, I mean (a) months or even years of intermittent prayer, or (b) up to eight hours of concentrated prayer at one time.[3]

This deliberate approach did not dampen people's interest in MacNutt's ministry at all. He was part of the group that founded the Charismatic Concerns Committee in the early 1970s (later renamed the Charismatic Leaders Fellowship), serving as its chairman for a number of years. He was a speaker at the ecumenical Conference on Charismatic Renewal in the Christian Churches in 1977, when fifty thousand people (half of them Catholics) filled Kansas City's Arrowhead Stadium. He was widely welcomed at events ranging from Lutheran to Pentecostal; in just a few years, he had ministered in 31 nations on five continents.

As his exposure broadened, he had to rethink certain customs—for example, who should be allowed to receive the Eucharist. At one Notre Dame conference, he listened to a sermon on John 6, where Jesus calls himself the Bread of Life.

But when it came time for the bread and the cup, the celebrant reminded Protestants in the audience (some 10 percent) that they should not approach the altar rail. MacNutt and a few others walked out.

"It was an awful way to handle it, especially after that gospel," he said. "If you have an ecumenical service, then don't have Communion. Have something else."[4]

An even more personal conundrum arose after he met a considerably younger clinical psychologist at a Jerusalem conference named Judith Sewell. She led a house of prayer in that city. Over the next few years, they felt more and more drawn to each other, which forced MacNutt to reassess his vow of celibacy. Did God really require him to remain single in order to continue his ministry?

Judith returned to the United States in 1977. Her heart for the healing of emotions and memories synchronized perfectly with Francis's emphasis. Years earlier, while working in a Boston hospital, one of her mentally ill patients had committed suicide. She had wept before God in frustration about her shortcomings as a counselor. In that moment, she had sensed God saying to her, *Bring them to Me. I will heal them.* Since that time, her ministry approach had greatly integrated the spiritual with the psychological.

In 1980, Francis, now 54 years old, flew to Chicago to ask the Dominican leader for a "dispensation," which would allow him to become a layman again so they could marry. Pope John Paul II ended up saying no. That led the National Service Committee of the Catholic Charismatic Renewal, of which he was a member, to express its dismay, calling his action "objectively, seriously wrong . . . a tremendous personal mistake."

Francis and Judith were nonetheless married in a quiet ceremony in Clearwater, Florida. His clerical collar was gone forever. They soon had a baby daughter named Rachel, then a son named David. And while some Catholic doors closed to them, new ones kept opening. They established something fresh called Christian Healing Ministries, Inc. (CHM), to pray for those in need and to teach others how to do the same. In 1987, the Episcopal bishop of Florida invited them to relocate CHM to Jacksonville, where it continues today.

And in 1993, the Catholic Church relented, granting Francis his long-delayed dispensation. The day came when the couple repeated their marriage vows in a ceremony before Bishop John Snyder of the Diocese of St. Augustine. By 2007, the Vatican's renewal office was even willing to co-sponsor a six-day conference with CHM that brought 450 Catholic leaders from 42 countries to Jacksonville for teaching on healing prayer.

Judith MacNutt's ministry has been widely welcomed like her husband's. The two of them co-authored a book entitled *Praying for Your Unborn Child*, published by Doubleday. She later wrote two on her own: *Angels Are for Real* and *Encountering Angels*. When she speaks these days, her mature insights and gentle style hold the interest of audiences as she says such things as "If you really want to get someone's attention, pray for them and let them be healed—and then proclaim Jesus." Her husband's legacy (he died at the age of 94) lives on in her work.

28

Bernard E. Underwood
(1925–1999) and
Ithiel Clemmons
(1921–1999)

The Reconcilers

O ne man grew up in the small towns of Virginia and West Virginia, the son of a Pentecostal Holiness pastor. The other man was a pastor's son, too—but grew up on the mean streets of Brooklyn, New York. Both inhaled the "Jim Crow" assumptions that black was black, white was white, and never the twain would meet, even though they prayed to the same God and hoped to please Him.

They both followed their fathers' footsteps into the ministry. Underwood served Appalachian churches, while Clemmons came alongside his father at Brooklyn's First Church of God in Christ. During those years, he also made time to complete an MA degree (City College of New York), plus a master of divinity at Union Seminary. By the 1960s, he was helping to map strategy for Dr. Martin Luther King Jr.'s civil rights work in the city and organizing the Foundation for Urban Ministries.

Meanwhile, Underwood was rising to more and more Pentecostal Holiness leadership posts on the state and then national level. This brought exposure to the Pentecostal Fellowship of North America (PFNA), of which his denomination was a charter member. Each year executives would come together to worship, pray, network and share ideas. It was an inspiring conclave.

Except . . . it was all white. The millions of African American Pentecostals had never been invited.

Underwood was elected his denomination's general superintendent in 1989. By the time he also became chairman of the PFNA two years later, he was convinced that things had to change. He reached out to Ithiel Clemmons in a spirit of repentance. Both bishops were painfully aware that, as Underwood summarized, "the manifestation of racial reconciliation survived at Azusa Street for about three years—from 1906 to 1909. But then they succumbed to the pressures of a racist culture rather than surrender to the gracious work of the Holy Spirit."[1] The two began to explore how the damage could be repaired.

Four exploratory meetings of leaders were held over the next two years, leading up to a formal conference in the fall of 1994, to be called "Pentecostal Partners: A Reconciliation Strategy for 21st-Century Ministry." The site would be Memphis, headquarters of Clemmons's denomination and, not incidentally, the city where a white man had gunned down Dr. King back in 1968.

Expectations ran high; more than three thousand attended the evening sessions in a large convention center. "Racism in the Pentecostal-charismatic community must be eradicated," Underwood declared in the opening session. "What a difference it would have made during the civil rights movement in America if all the children of the Pentecostal revival had stood together."

For his part, Clemmons led the way in drafting a manifesto that included such statements as:

> I pledge in concert with my brothers and sisters of many hues to oppose racism prophetically in all its various manifestations within and without the Body of Christ and to be vigilant in the struggle. . . .
>
> We commit ourselves not only to pray but also to work for genuine and visible manifestations of Christian unity. . . .[2]

The breakthrough moment came not in an evening meeting, but rather in an afternoon session for scholars. When Church of God in Christ bishop Charles E. Blake voiced a tearful commitment to love in spite of the many problems, a spirit of weeping and repentance seemed to sweep the room. A young black man raised his voice in an utterance of tongues. Immediately, noted Foursquare pastor Jack Hayford (white) gave the lengthy interpretation, beginning:

> For the Lord would speak to you this day . . . My sons and daughters, look, if you will, from the heavenward side of things, and see where you have been two separate streams—that is, streams as at floodtide. For I have poured out of my Spirit upon you and flooded you with grace in both your circles of gathering and fellowship.
>
> But . . . the waters have been muddied to some degree. . . . You have not been aware of it. . . .
>
> But look! Look, for I, by my Spirit, am flowing the two streams into one. And the two becoming one, if you can see from the heaven side of things, are being purified. . . .[3]

The listeners were still absorbing this interpretation when Donald Evans, a white Assemblies of God pastor from the South (Tampa, FL) appeared at the edge of the stage holding a basin of water and a towel. He said the Lord had impressed him to wash the feet of a black leader as a sign of repentance. Soon he was kneeling in front of Ithiel Clemmons, washing his feet and begging forgiveness for the sins of whites against their black brothers and sisters. The entire audience began to weep afresh.

The next thing to happen was Bishop Blake asking to wash the feet of Thomas Trask, general superintendent of the (largely white) Assemblies of God. He said it was in repentance for any animosity blacks harbored against their white counterparts.

The old die had been shattered; a new die was being cast. By the next afternoon's business session, the all-white PFNA had been dissolved, and a new constitution was being drafted for the PCCNA—Pentecostal/Charismatic Churches of North America—with full representation on its board and membership of denominations and groups regardless of color. Chairing the new board would be Bishop Clemmons, with his friend Bishop Underwood as vice-chair. The PCCNA continues today as a much larger, more vigorous fellowship with triple the number of members as the old group.

Clemmons was realistic enough to take note of strong feelings below the surface. A one-and-done conference would not be enough. "When whites draw near blacks, there is often fear," he explained. "There is a fear of a loss of autonomy." He went on to outline the practical steps that lead to genuine reconciliation:

1. *Celebration* (worshiping together), of course. But then comes . . .

2. *Conversation*—telling personal stories of how we woke up to our racial assumptions

3. *Confession*—admitting past and present sins

4. *Cooperation* on projects we can undertake together

5. Thereafter, being willing to engage in *criticism*, pointing out areas that still need attention

6. And finally, back to *worship*[4]

In the quarter century since the "Memphis Miracle," as it came to be called, not all racial problems have been solved. But the forward path that B. E. Underwood and Ithiel Clemmons pioneered is being pursued by their heirs, to the enrichment of all components of the Spirit-empowered church.

29

Larry Christenson
(1928–2017)

A Leader for Lutherans

In 1962, a panel of three professionals arrived in San Pedro, California, to investigate just what was going on at Trinity Lutheran Church. The psychiatrist, the clinical psychologist, and the New Testament theologian would interview the young pastor, Larry Christenson, and several dozen church members who, according to rumor, had gotten swept up in something very un-Lutheran: speaking in tongues. Hadn't the great Reformer himself, Martin Luther, frowned upon the *Schwärmer* ("enthusiasts") of his day, who claimed to receive direct words from the Holy Spirit?

Christenson, a graduate of solidly orthodox St. Olaf College in his native Minnesota, had finished up at Luther Theological Seminary only two years before. But along the way, he had read Agnes Sanford's book *The Healing Light*, which had raised enough curiosity for him to drop by a revival meeting at a nearby Foursquare church. The sermon that Thursday night dealt with the baptism in the Holy Spirit. He received the evangelist's prayer at the end, but nothing seemed to happen.

However, in the wee hours of the morning, he said he sat bolt upright in bed and found an unknown tongue hovering on his lips. He spoke a sentence in tongues . . . and then fell back asleep. The next night, he returned to the Foursquare church, where "a great sense of praise began to well up within me, and it spilled over my lips in a new tongue." He found it to be a wonderful experience, "though not a particularly overwhelming one."[1]

In the following days, a cloud came across his mind: Was this suitable for a Lutheran? Should he remain a Lutheran minister? A timely conversation with charismatic emissary David du Plessis persuaded him to stay put. As he conveyed what had happened to his congregation, men and women began to receive what he was describing.

When the visiting panel came, the Trinity Lutheran folk proved not to be as eccentric as feared. Dr. Paul Qualben, a psychiatrist, reported at a seminary event a decade later:

> We had two preconceptions when we went. . . . We expected to encounter people who were emotionally unstable, and we expected the phenomenon to be short-lived. We were wrong on both counts. The people we interviewed were a normal cross-section of a Lutheran congregation, and today, ten years later, the movement is still growing.[2]

Indeed, it was, thanks in part to the steady credibility of Larry Christenson. He was not flamboyant; he didn't make outlandish claims; he simply helped shepherd the growing numbers of Lutherans across the nation who were eager for new spiritual life. Some of his fellow charismatic pastors were excommunicated, but many others maintained their ordination in their church and joined Christenson in the work. When the first International Lutheran Conference on the Holy Spirit convened in 1972 at the Minneapolis Civic Auditorium, more than nine thousand people showed up.

That led soon after to an ongoing organization called Lutheran Charismatic Renewal Services. When the big cross-denominational gathering in Kansas City happened in 1977, Lutherans comprised the third-largest group of registrants. "It [Spirit baptism] is a common experience that opens the way to unity," Christenson observed. "With that comes an adherence to Scripture as the final authority. I've never heard an argument about the Virgin Birth or the divinity of Christ at Charismatic conferences. We're very keenly aware of theological differences, but we don't see that as hindering places where we have agreement."[3]

Lutheranism, of course, has always taken its theology seriously, ever since the days of championing justification by faith in the 1500s. Now its charismatic awakening spawned many colloquia, study groups of academics and committee reports. Christenson's book *The Charismatic Renewal Among Lutherans* (1976) was followed the next year by *Welcome, Holy Spirit: A Study of Charismatic Renewal in the Church*, published by the Lutheran publishing house Augsburg and edited by Christenson. Some forty scholars contributed. Such collaboration tended to dampen earlier skepticism such as that voiced back in 1972 by one Lutheran denomination (Missouri Synod) that "power and renewal are to be sought in the Word and sacraments, not in special signs and miracles." A parallel body, the Lutheran Church in America, had declared in its 1974 report

161

that "there is no cause for Lutheran pastors or people to suggest either explicitly or implicitly that one cannot be charismatic and remain a Lutheran in good standing."

Larry Christenson avoided many theological battles by advancing what he called an "organic view" of the baptism with the Holy Spirit. Rather than echoing standard Pentecostal language about tongues being the "initial physical evidence" of the Spirit's fullness, he wrote in *Trinity* magazine that he had undertaken his own review of the Acts narratives and concluded:

> Does this mean that everyone who receives the Holy Spirit will speak in tongues—that if you have not spoken in tongues you have not really received the Holy Spirit? I do not believe you can make such a case from Scripture. However, I do believe that the book of Acts suggests to us a helpful *pattern:* 1) Receiving the Holy Spirit is a definite, clear-cut, instantaneous experience. . . . 2) A simple and God-appointed way for you objectively to manifest the gift of the Holy Spirit is to lift up your voice in faith, and speak out in a new tongue at the prompting of the Holy Spirit.[4]

In 1983, after nearly a quarter century at his California pastorate, Christenson and his wife, Nordis, returned to their Twin Cities roots so he could become the full-time director of the International Lutheran Renewal Center. He served in this leadership role for twelve years. His books continued to sell, especially his Gold Medallion–winning classic, *The Christian Family* (two million sold to date), which had led the way in marriage-and-parenting titles; it first appeared back in 1970, years before Dr. James Dobson started Focus on the Family (1977) and other specialties arose.

Christenson's 1968 book, *Speaking in Tongues*, remains in print today as well. The Christian Research Institute called it "an excellent study on this gift: whether you agree or disagree, this book will answer many questions people are asking today."

Thus, whether focusing on spiritual awakening or family relationships, he was a pacesetter, a source of wisdom, a counsel to many and a treasure to the many-faceted Body of Christ.

30

Pat Robertson
(1930–)

The Busy Media Magnate

I f you went to a library looking for a biography of Pat Robertson, what sections would you check?

Entrepreneurs? He certainly made his mark in the business world, taking a defunct UHF television station in Portsmouth, Virginia, in 1959 and turning it into a nationwide religious cable network. Even that wasn't his pinnacle; he began adding wholesome entertainment shows into something called the CBN Family Channel (63 million subscribers) that, after several name changes, was eventually sold for $136.1 million—provided it would keep airing his daily hourlong flagship show, *The 700 Club*, no matter who owned it.

University founders? Robertson's Regent University in Virginia Beach opened in 1977, growing steadily to a student body today of ten thousand students pursuing fully accredited programs in everything from health care to law to business to theology at bachelor's, master's and doctorate levels. Its twenty thousand alumni hail from 84 nations. (Robertson himself earned his bachelor's degree *magna cum laude* at Washington and Lee University in 1950, where he was Phi Beta Kappa; he then followed with a law degree from Yale in 1955.)

Clergy? Soon after graduating from the Biblical Seminary of New York (now New York Theological Seminary) in 1959, he was ordained as a Southern Baptist, the church of his family heritage. He kept this ordination until 1987, when he resigned in order to run for president.

Politicians? He grew up in that climate as the son of a long-serving United States senator, A. Willis Robertson (D-Va.). In his own right, Pat served on President Ronald Reagan's Task Force on Victims of Crime. His boldest venture came in 1986, when he announced he would seek the US presidency as a Republican if three million registered voters signed petitions for him to do so over the next twelve months. No problem. When the primary elections began, he won the states of Hawaii, Alaska and Washington; he came in a strong second in both Iowa and Michigan. Eventually he stepped back to endorse the ultimate winner, Vice President George H. W. Bush.

Grassroots organizers? His Christian Coalition, formed in 1989, used the remainder of his campaign money to mobilize voters. It distributed millions of "voter guides" to churches and other outlets during subsequent election seasons.

Justice activists? Becoming concerned about the efforts of the ACLU and other liberal lobby groups, Robertson developed the American Center for Law and Justice (ACLJ) in 1990 to help defend constitutional freedoms and conservative values, especially human life. It has sometimes won cases even before the US Supreme Court.

Humanitarians? His Operation Blessing organization was activated as far back as 1978 to provide medical, hunger and disaster relief not only in the United States but also around the world. Its projects run the gamut from orphan care to clean water installations to small-business development—a $276-million-per-year effort in all.

Private investors? His financial interests over the years have ranged from international banking services to Asian media companies to African gold and diamond mines to thoroughbred racehorses.

Authors? He is the author of at least eighteen books, including what *Time* magazine called the number-one religious book of 1984, *The Secret Kingdom: Your Path to Peace, Love, and Financial Security.*

No wonder Auburn University scholar David Harrell gave a whole chapter of his 384-page Robertson biography to what he titled "Multiple Incarnations."[1] The man's life and work does not fit into one small cubicle. But he will always be known best for his laid-back, genial style as the daily host of *The 700 Club* (the name comes from an early fund-raising telethon, when he sought seven hundred viewers to pledge ten dollars a month, thereby covering the modest seven-thousand-dollar monthly operating budget at the time; the name has stuck ever since).

On air, he does not raise his voice or wave his arms; he does not even stand up from behind the desk. Why do people keep watching and supporting the show, now more than sixty years running? Three features stand out:

1. *Robertson's interviews with leading voices* across the Pentecostal and charismatic landscape. The guest list over the years includes many who went on to establish

their own media outreaches. Hardly a prominent evangelist or Bible teacher has not benefited from this nationwide platform.

2. *Inspiring field reports* of credible miracles of healing. Nearly every day's show includes one if not two well-filmed stories of someone, often at death's door, who was brought back to health through the power of God. Viewers cannot help finding hope for their own needs as they watch.

3. *Personalized, direct prayer for needs in real time.* Every day Robertson looks straight into the camera, gives a short word of encouragement, then closes his eyes and boldly asks God to intervene in the viewer's difficulty. This often includes one or more Spirit-led "words of knowledge"—and not just quick generic mentions such as "arthritis" or "lower back pain." Here is a sample from the telecast of March 25, 2020:

> There's a little girl—I believe the name is Emily—and you've broken your arm. And it's very painful. And right now, you're going to feel a warmth in that break, and those bones are knitting together miraculously. And your arm is completely well.

When this kind of thing is aired regarding a child, a man, a woman or anyone, feedback (phone or email) arrives in a few days from the individual (or their family member). They happily tell about quick relief and often cite doctor verification.

Meanwhile, viewers can initiate their own requests for prayer by calling the easy-to-remember toll-free number, 1-800-700-7000, where banks of phone counselors hear their pleas and pray with them immediately. A recent year tallied 1.9 million inbound calls. Some fourteen thousand people made professions of faith that year while still on the line.

Yes, some Christians second-guess Robertson's choice of guests. Critics find fault with some of his on-air commentaries about events in the news—for example, that the devastating Hurricane Katrina (2005) might be God's punishment for America's abortion policy. They keep track of his predictions that failed to come true; one example in 2012 was that Mitt Romney would win the election against Barack Obama and become a two-term president. Terry Meeuwsen, Robertson's longtime co-host, says with a smile, "He's a lion made to roar."[2] His assertions (and how they are phrased) will never please everyone.

Still, there is no denying that the long ministry of Pat Robertson through television across as many as 159 nations in seventy languages, plus publishing, film-making, benevolent aid and higher education, has impacted the lives of millions for good.

31

Everett L. "Terry" Fullam
(1930–2014)

New Life for an Old Mold

The well-heeled parishioners of St. Mark's Episcopal Church in Darien, Connecticut—perhaps the wealthiest town along the state's "Gold Coast"—thought they knew what they were getting when Terry Fullam arrived as their new rector in October 1972. His academic record, leading up to a master's degree in philosophy from Harvard (*magna cum laude,* no less), was strong; he had the bishop's endorsement; he was now 42 years old; the vote to call him had been unanimous; and at six-foot-three, he certainly looked the part.

"This morning, as I start my ministry among you," the man in the long black cassock, white surplice and slim green stole said that first Sunday, "I must ask for your prayers. For I come in the assurance that this is the Lord's call as well as your own. It is certainly my prayer that God will, in our time together,

169

mold us and make us according to his will."[1] The worshipers nodded in approval.

A week later, however, brought some surprises, as Fullam got more specific: "I think it is important for all of us to realize something," he intoned in a steady voice. "In the coming months, one of two things will happen to each of you. Either you will find yourself opening up more and more to the Lord, in which case you will be growing and expanding in your relationship with him, and you will know it—or else you will find yourself constricting and tightening, in which case the atmosphere will become intolerable." People held their breath . . . just whatever did he mean?

Without a touch of harshness, he added realistically, "Some of you will find it necessary to go."[2]

A few might have left the church, but they were quickly replaced by newcomers drawn to listen to the articulate, biblically grounded rector. The Wednesday night Bible study outgrew the parish hall and had to be moved to the sanctuary. A Sunday evening prayer-and-praise meeting, largely attended by youth, had to move to a larger Episcopal church in nearby Stamford. A Tuesday morning gathering for worship, teaching, sharing and Communion surged to some 250 attenders, mostly women, packing out the sanctuary. Bible studies in homes seemed to sprout everywhere. Troubled marriages were restored, healings reported.

Sunday morning attendance shot up from 250 to 1,200 in five years—not in the Bible Belt, but here in cool, sophisticated New England. Two of the four Sunday services had to move to a nearby high school to accommodate the crowds. Said the bishop of Connecticut, "Whatever you're doing, don't stop."[3]

Phil March, an advertising executive and a lay reader in the church, made this observation:

What we had . . . was the traditional people coming to the Lord and getting baptized in the Holy Spirit[4]—the people who had sort of played around in the Episcopal church most of their lives—they more or less figured, "Well, we've got it all" and then they discovered something was lacking and Fullam was able to help them find it. . . .

And, of course, you had the new people coming at the same time, the people who had really wanted nothing to do with an established church, but who were finding that this guy was making good sense. . . . And then they got zapped, and before you knew it, they were coming because they really wanted to.[5]

But it was not just a case of Fullam magic. "I am *not* the head of this church," he said repeatedly. "I can't build this church. I haven't the foggiest idea how to do it. But the Lord knows how, and He will do it if we just submit ourselves to Him. He is perfectly capable of building His own church."[6]

He was so convinced of this that he persuaded the vestry (governing board) to adopt a radical idea: All decisions going forward would be unanimous. In other words, no more "majority rule." If on a given matter there was even one dissenting vote, that simply meant the group did not yet have the mind of the Lord. They should pause for more reflection and prayer. And in case after case, this proved to be the path of wisdom. "Jesus can run the church," Fullam kept insisting.

When a magazine editor flew from Chicago in 1984 for an interview, he noticed an architect's model of a large sanctuary sitting off in a corner, gathering dust. What was this? the editor asked.

"That's what we thought God wanted us to build five or six years ago, when our present building first filled up," Fullam answered. "You know, the place was packed, we were having four morning services—time to build a bigger barn. It was going to go right out on the front lawn.

"But when we went to the city fathers for approval, they said NO. Our plans would be a massive overdevelopment of this wooded area, they ruled."

Out of that disappointment came an alternate vision through the church's senior warden: "God wants us instead to build the living church, to give ourselves to strengthening his people not only here in Darien, but across the nation and even the world."[7]

That is, indeed, what happened. The church began holding semiannual Parish Renewal Weekends, drawing earnest leaders from various quarters, three hundred at a time. Fullam was endorsed by the vestry to take more outside speaking invitations to large clergy and diocesan conferences across the nation. He became president of a network called Episcopal Renewal Ministries.

Finally, after 27 years at St. Paul's, he resigned his post in 1989 to travel even more widely, ultimately touching more than 25 countries.

His perspective was perhaps best summarized as follows:

My vision for the church today is of three streams leading into one river. From the historic Protestant side comes the emphasis on the Word, the priesthood of the believer, and the need for individual, personal encounter with God. From the Catholic stream comes the idea of the corporate body of Christ—that you can't be a Christian all by yourself. . . . So here I learn the need for mutual submission.

Then the third stream is the charismatic dimension, which emphasizes the immediacy of God's working in our lives. The operation of the Spirit does not supplant the Scripture in any way, but it shows that God still speaks to us today, through prophecy and in other ways as well.

So my personal quest is for wholeness, for moving from a partial to a more adequate understanding of the vision. . . . The church as I see it needs to be Catholic, Protestant, and charismatic all at once.[8]

32

C. Peter Wagner
(1930–2016)

Riding the Waves

No, thank you. The young missionary to Bolivia wanted no part of oddball Pentecostalism, as he viewed it. The sending agencies under which he served were members in good standing with the Interdenominational Foreign Missions Association, which required each mission to "maintain a non-charismatic orientation."

". . . I was a dispensationalist who carried a Scofield [Reference] Bible," Peter Wagner said, "and could construct all the charts from memory. I recall very clearly that when a faith healer came to our city of Cochabamba, Bolivia, I warned our Bolivian believers not to go to the meetings and wrote an article for the national evangelical magazine refuting his claims."[1]

Then a couple of events jostled his dogma. E. Stanley Jones, the renowned Methodist evangelist, came to his city. Wagner and his wife, Doris, were wary of "liberal" theology but went to hear him anyway, intentionally arriving late and sitting in the back. It turned out to be a healing service. Wagner was not about to go forward for prayer—but when he awakened the next morning, the open, festering cyst on his neck (which was scheduled for a second surgery) had suddenly dried up.

Not long afterward, he traveled to neighboring Chile to do research on a subject dear to his heart: church growth. His appetite had been whetted by his mentor, Dr. Donald McGavran, founding dean of the School of World Mission at Fuller Theological Seminary, where Wagner had earned his master of divinity degree.

> If nothing else, [I] was attracted by the phenomenal growth of the Chilean Pentecostal churches. There I witnessed healings, speaking in tongues, concert prayers, baptisms in the Spirit, dancing in the Spirit, prophecies, visions—just as if they were a normal part of 20th-century Christian experience.
>
> So fascinated did I become that I [later] wrote a book called *What Are We Missing?*[2] describing what God is doing in Latin American Pentecostalism.[3]

This did not mean that the Wagners abruptly shifted theological gears. Following sixteen years of missionary service, Peter took up a faculty position at his California alma mater in 1971, where he would teach for the next three decades. The couple joined nearby Lake Avenue Congregational Church. Peter still carried his Scofield Bible and considered himself "just a straight-line evangelical."[4]

But for the next thirty years at Fuller—and another decade after that—Wagner's voice and pen kept challenging the Christian community's assumptions. He would be no quiet ivory-tower professor. He sincerely wanted to spotlight spiritual activity in the contemporary setting, and could wax into grand rhetoric (sometimes hyperbole?) while creating his more than seventy books. He made some people cheer, others squirm.

In the 1970s, he and McGavran ignited the "Church Growth" emphasis, seeking to make congregations more effective in evangelism. They observed sociologically that human beings prefer to associate with others like themselves—which they dubbed the "homogeneous-unit principle." Wagner wrote a book entitled *Our Kind of People*,[5] which generated a lot of buzz among pastors. He was not trying to give congregations a license to stay segregated by race or economic class (after all, he'd been a cross-cultural missionary himself), but that is what some heard regardless.

Debates sprang up about whether churches needed to become "seeker-sensitive." Some Pentecostal churches actually began suppressing the verbal gifts of the Spirit on Sunday mornings.

Church growth would be accelerated, Wagner believed, by activating the members' *other* spiritual gifts. His bestseller *Your Spiritual Gifts Can Help Your Church Grow* (1979) was quickly followed by an innovative questionnaire (137 questions) that people could use to identify which of the 28 *charismata* mentioned in Scripture might be theirs.[6]

By the beginning of the 1980s, Wagner turned to another turbocharger for church growth: signs and wonders. He had gotten acquainted with a nearby pastor, John Wimber (Vineyard Christian Fellowship, Anaheim, California), who had become an adjunct professor at Fuller. Together, they conceived and got permission to co-teach a Monday night course called "Signs, Wonders and Church Growth" that not only lectured on the topic but included in-class "ministry time," when students put into practice what they had learned about praying for the sick.

The results were dramatic—healings, words of knowledge, prophecies. Attendance grew so large the course had to be moved to the seminary's largest classroom. Fuller's sizable portion of international students said this was just normal Christianity, based on what they had practiced in their home countries. The North Americans, on the other hand, were amazed. *Christian Life* magazine ran a full issue (October 1982) on the awakening. President David Allan Hubbard wrote: "For 35 years at Fuller Seminary we have sought both to teach the tenets of Biblical faith as interpreted by the reformers and to be open to the experiences and contributions of the current movement of the Holy Spirit which came into prominence about the turn of our century. The course . . . is an expression of our long-term interest in preserving a Biblical balance between the extremes. Hazarding the risks of this approach to the life of the Spirit is part of what Fuller is prepared to do."[7]

The course continued to be offered from 1982 to 1985, then was blended into another course called "The Ministry of Healing in World Evangelization."

By 1988, Wagner had constructed a historical framework that he expressed in another book, *The Third Wave of the Holy Spirit: Encountering the Power of Signs and Wonders Today.* His three "waves" were (1) the classical Pentecostal outpouring that started at the Azusa Street Mission in 1906, (2) the charismatic awakening in mainline churches (Protestant and Catholic) beginning around 1960, and now (3) the "signs and wonders" surge, similar to the first two but different in some ways (for example, he affirmed no distinct "baptism in the Holy Spirit").

In the 1990s, Wagner's attention shifted to combating the resistance of Satan and his demons—what he called "spiritual warfare." His new books, *Confronting the Powers* and

Engaging the Enemy, again employed a three-tiered construct: (1) Ground Level, resisting the devil's everyday temptations, (2) Occult Level, casting out demonic forces someone might have absorbed through witchcraft, astrology or satanic contact, and (3) Strategic Level, which theorized that certain "principalities and powers" ruled over certain cities or regions of the world as "territorial spirits" and needed to be ousted.

Many readers recognized the reality of the first level, even accepted the need for the second, but harbored uncertainties about the third.[8]

The 1990s brought a return to the matter of spiritual giftings, particularly the role of modern-day apostles and prophets. Wagner heralded what he termed a "New Apostolic Reformation" (NAR), wrote a book called *Apostles Today*[9] and helped found an International Coalition of Apostolic Leaders in 1999. He served as its Presiding Apostle for eight years, defining the 21st century as a Second Apostolic Age (the first being in the first century AD). Membership in the NAR was by invitation only. Wagner had to defend this informal network against charges of being a cult.

In his 2008 book, *Dominion! How Kingdom Action Can Change the World*, he called these apostles and others ("workplace apostles") to "a paradigm shift to the Church's approach to salvation and societal change."[10] This involved taking authority over the "Seven Mountains" of culture: education, religion, family, business, government/military, arts/entertainment and media.

When he passed away at age 86, a solidly Southern Baptist acquaintance (Dr. Ed Stetzer, executive director of Wheaton College's Billy Graham Center) wrote in an online tribute, "If you knew Peter Wagner, people would often ask, 'Which Peter

Wagner?' They asked not because he was two-faced, but because he changed his views so much. . . . He was a friend to many of us, even when we disagreed with *early* Peter and/or *later* Peter! He was always a kind voice, looking for how God was at work, and seeking to celebrate what he saw as the move of the Spirit."[11]

33

Michael Harper
(1931–2010)

Forks in the Road

Expectations ran high in Michael Harper's parents that he, following a proper education, would carry on in the family business of wholesaling food to the London grocery and restaurant industries. He studied at two elite private schools before entering Emmanuel College, Cambridge, on a scholarship in 1950 to pursue law. When asked during an initial interview with the dean what church he belonged to, he could not think of the name. "Oh—er, the usual," he blurted. Religion was hardly at the front of his mind.

But then, something odd happened one Sunday morning. At a friend's suggestion, he dropped into the King's College Chapel during a Communion service already underway.

> For the first time in my life I felt the touch of God. There is nothing on earth to compare with that glorious experience when you know that you have passed into the safe hands of Christ. . . .

The Holy Spirit had been working on me for several weeks, and I had been discovering that even some of my virtues were vices. But now things had been put right. I was in the clear. How comforting were the bread and wine to me that morning.[1]

He immediately began attending Christian Union meetings and building friendships. Soon he was reading Christian books and developing a personal life of devotion. After two years of college, he switched his major from law to theology. "My parents were confused; they thought I had become infected with religious mania,"[2] he wrote later. When he announced that he wanted to continue after graduation by enrolling at Ridley Hall, Cambridge's ministerial school, his disappointed father frowned and said if his son really was going to take this fork in the road, he hoped he would end up as the Archbishop of Canterbury!

Spiritual fervor was running high at Ridley Hall during those years, especially when evangelist Billy Graham came to London in 1954. Michael Harper was ordained into the Church of England the next year, and a year later married his wife, Jeanne. After an initial position in Battersea, they came in 1958 to the wellspring of evangelical life in the Anglican world, All Souls Church, Langham Place, London, where the noteworthy John R. W. Stott had just been appointed rector. Harper's assignment, as one of six curates, was to reach out to five large Oxford Street department stores nearby as a kind of "business chaplain." He spent hours on the sales floors chatting with staff, and also organized a weekly lunch-hour service for employees as well as their bosses. He and Jeanne were happy.

But when it came to preaching, he did not see the response he hoped for. People listened politely, then headed out with little comment. He sensed that for all his careful sermon preparation, the power of the Gospel was missing. It bothered him for a long time.

In May 1962, a friend invited him to speak at a weekend conference outside the city. He sat down to prepare five talks from the book of Ephesians. The longer he worked, the more Paul's two prayers (1:17–23 and 3:14–21) began to come alive.

> The first prayer is for "revelation" not "head knowledge", and there is a world of difference between the two! The words that are used in this passage express this—"wisdom", "revelation", "knowledge", "the eyes of the heart", "enlightened". The whole prayer may be summarized in the words—*that you may know.* . . . Paul was not praying for intellectual knowledge. Rather, Paul is praying that his fellow Christians in Ephesus would have the kind of knowledge that is supernaturally inspired, and that was something I knew very little about in personal experience.[3]

The longer he worked on his messages, both at home and on the train to the conference, the more excited he became. The weekend sessions turned out to be powerfully effective. He could hardly wait to get back to Jeanne and give his glowing report. A few weeks later, she received an equivalent awakening of spiritual life and passion, and from that point onward, their walk with God moved ahead briskly. They considered all this to be their baptism in the Holy Spirit, although without any speaking in tongues ("a complete red herring,"[4] said Michael, "beneath the dignity of an Anglican minister"[5]).

Just then news of the fledgling charismatic movement in America was drifting across the Atlantic. The Harpers could not help noticing how many Episcopalians (fellow Anglicans) were involved. Closer at hand, a faithful architect in the All

Souls congregation said he had been baptized in the Spirit and spoken in tongues while in his bathtub! How had this come about, pray tell? He said he had gone to a meeting to hear David du Plessis, who had advised him to choose a relaxing environment as he waited for the Spirit.

The man passed along his copy of *Trinity*, a charismatic magazine spawned out of Fr. Dennis Bennett's Episcopal church in California, which intrigued Michael and Jeanne more than ever. They went back to reexamine what the book of Acts actually reported about tongues. They had not noticed that even Mary, the mother of the Lord, spoke in tongues along with the rest on the Day of Pentecost (1:14). Their hesitations began to melt away.

In the summer of 1963, the American Lutheran leader Larry Christenson and his wife, Nordis, were passing through London on their way home from a conference in Finland, and the Harpers invited them to stay in their home. When the calm, respectable guest asked Michael if he had spoken in tongues yet, he replied, "No—but I want to." Christenson followed with some practical instructions, then dropped the subject.

Another American guest was sharing the hospitality of the Harpers' small flat as well, so that . . .

> . . . Jeanne and I found ourselves sleeping in the living room. Jeanne slept on the sofa, and I was on the floor; the nearest I've yet got to becoming a "holy roller." I found sleep difficult that night. For one thing it wasn't exactly comfortable. For another my mind was preoccupied. . . . "Was I on the right track? Was this not a dangerous and divisive movement? Was I not leading many people astray? What would my friends be thinking of me? What about my future?"
>
> Around the middle of the night I remembered all that Larry had said to me. "Try it; begin to speak; don't speak English,"

and so on. So I tried. Maybe for a split second there were some man-made sounds. I forget. But almost instantly I was speaking a new language. As I did so, two wonderful things happened all at once. The Lord seemed to take two steps forward. He had seemed a little out of touch. Now He was really close. And secondly those worries and fear evaporated. And here I was, not in any state of ecstasy (I defy anyone to feel ecstatic lying on a hard floor!), but speaking to God with a freedom and joy I had always wanted to, and never quite found possible. My mind was unclouded, and fully aware of what was going on. It was a most glorious sensation of perfect communication between God and man.[6]

Soon thereafter, Harper began setting up meetings for the next time Christenson returned to the UK, and for other charismatics as well, including du Plessis. He arranged to reprint two thousand copies of Christenson's booklet *Speaking in Tongues, a Gift for the Body of Christ*. People began writing and asking for tape recordings as well. For the Harpers, life got busier than ever.

He gradually came to realize that his work as an All Souls curate no longer held first place in his heart. Once again, there was a fork in his road. The honest thing to do would be to step out into something new—but what? How? He finally made an appointment in February 1964 to sit down with his rector. In his book, he wrote:

It is common knowledge that John Stott did not share these views of the work of the Holy Spirit. There was a very real difference in theology, but throughout that period there was a continued unity in other ways. John Stott never suggested or even hinted that I should leave All Souls, which is much to his credit since he was receiving some pressure from others to do this. . . . I shall always be grateful for the impeccable way he acted under these difficult circumstances. . . .

By mutual agreement I was to stay on until June, thus completing just over six years at All Souls. In the meantime the idea of the Fountain Trust, as it was later called, was forming in my mind.[7]

This new charity became the nerve center for charismatic publications and conferences across the British Isles, with Harper serving as its director for the next eleven years. It was not a formal organization per se; it had no membership. Instead, it simply gave voice to what the Holy Spirit was doing across many sectors of Christendom. Its *Renewal* magazine provided a steady stream of credible testimonies and thoughtful teaching.

In one issue, Harper wrote, "It was when Protestant believers saw Roman Catholics filled with the Spirit and speaking in tongues that they knew they had to extend the hand of fellowship. We could not reject those whom God clearly regarded as his children."[8] His travels to other parts of Europe and even farther (America, Canada, Australia, New Zealand, Singapore, several African nations) for at least twenty years brought life and wisdom to Spirit-hungry audiences.

In 1984, he finally settled down to become canon of Chichester Cathedral on the south coast of England. A decade later, he moved his ordination from Anglican to Orthodox out of concern for doctrinal fidelity. But he never stopped advocating for the Holy Spirit to have His way, even in the most liturgical settings. "The Lord is coming for a prepared Church," he had written, "but he is not coming back for a small coterie of charismatics who are too impatient to wait for the rest of the Church. He is preparing the Church for his return. The renewal is well under way; but there is still much to be done."[9]

34

David Wilkerson
(1931–2011)

The Straight Shooter

The epic story has now gone around the world: A naïve, small-town Pennsylvania pastor browses *Life* magazine late one night in 1958 and sees a courtroom sketch of seven New York City gang members on trial for murdering a fifteen-year-old polio victim in a park. He thinks God is calling him to take the Gospel to those hardened, bitter teens. He begins driving into the city on his weekly day off, with no strategy for getting started.

David Wilkerson's eventual book *The Cross and the Switchblade* (written five years later with the masterful help of John and Elizabeth Sherrill) tells in heart-stopping detail how he tried unsuccessfully to meet the seven defendants. Blocked by court officials, he kept walking the mean streets, praying for guidance, seeing the devastation of heroin usage and trying to strike up conversations. One of the most dramatic was the day in Brooklyn's Fort Greene area when he first encountered Nicky Cruz, vice president of the vicious Dragons gang:

> I remember thinking, as I looked at him, that's the hardest face I have ever seen.
>
> "How do you do, Nicky," I said.
>
> He left me standing with my hand outstretched. He wouldn't even look at me. He was puffing away at a cigarette, shooting nervous little jets of smoke out the side of his mouth.
>
> "Go to hell, Preacher," he said. He had an odd, strangled way of speaking and he stuttered badly over some of his sounds.
>
> "You don't think much of me, Nicky," I said, "but I feel different about you. I love you, Nicky." I took a step toward him.
>
> "You come near me, Preacher," he said, in that tortured voice, "I'll kill you."
>
> "You could do that," I agreed. "You could cut me in a thousand pieces and lay them out on the street and every piece would love you."[1]

But with persistence, tough thugs (and their equally tough girlfriends) began softening to Wilkerson's message of grace and forgiveness. He and his wife, Gwen, eventually resigned their comfortable pastorate and moved into New York City with their three young children to found the ministry we know today as Teen Challenge. One of their best helpers turned out to be Nicky Cruz. A local board came together, starting with Wilkerson's Assemblies of God colleagues but soon adding Baptists, Presbyterians and Episcopalians. They banded together to pray for the light of Christ to break through the gloom of drug addiction and violence. Some of them even asked their business friends for funding help; as a result, a large house on Clinton

Avenue was purchased, cleaned up and turned into a center for hope and recovery.

Understandably, not every convert lasted. More than a few times, a young man would set out to follow Christ, move into the center, go through "cold turkey" withdrawal from heroin . . . and then disappear. Wilkerson and his team held high hopes for one young man who seemed to be doing well, until he said he wanted to go pay a quick visit to his parents.

> It came time for him to return. No Joe.
> The next morning we learned that our Joe had been arrested for robbery and for possession of narcotics.
> That was our failure. "What went wrong?" I asked at a staff meeting. "The boy went through the rough part. He got all the way through the worst three days he would ever have to spend. He had a tremendous investment to protect. And he threw it all over."[2]

Wilkerson began interviewing young men in the program.

> I spoke to Nicky, who had [originally] been taking goof balls[3] and smoking marijuana. I asked him when it was that he felt he had victory over his old way of life. Something tremendous had happened to him, he said, at the time of his conversion on the street corner. He had been introduced at that time to the love of God. But it wasn't until later that he knew he had complete victory.
> "And when was that, Nicky?"
> "At the time of my baptism in the Holy Spirit."
> I called in [another young man named] David and asked him the same thing. When did he feel that he had power over himself? "Oh, I can answer that," said David. "When I was baptized in the Holy Spirit."
> Again and again I got the same report.[4]

This dimension of inner power caught the attention of more than just needy teenagers. A Jesuit priest from Fordham University came to visit for much of a day. He heard testimonies from both guys and girls who had changed. "We still get tempted," one of them said, "but now we always run to the chapel and pray." For those in heightened need of a supporting atmosphere, a Teen Challenge Training Center was opened 150 miles outside the city, providing a five- to eight-month intensive residential plunge into Bible study, prayer and Holy Spirit overhaul. A 1976 independent survey of Teen Challenge graduates showed 71 percent were still "clean" when interviewed—a far higher number than secular or government programs were seeing.

Wilkerson wrote in his book:

> Certainly we cannot claim a magical cure for drug addiction. The devil which hides in that needle is so deadly strong that any such claim would be folly. All we can say, perhaps, is that we have found a power which captures a boy more strongly than narcotics. But that power is the Holy Spirit Himself which, unlike narcotics, does a strange thing for our boys: He captures only to liberate.[5]

The bestselling book lit flames of curiosity far beyond New York. Students at Duquesne University read it and became hungry for the kind of spiritual dynamic it described. Out of this grew the first Catholic charismatic prayer meeting in 1967, from which an entire movement was born. Teen Challenge centers opened in Chicago, Boston, Los Angeles, San Francisco and other needy cities. When a feature movie with the same title as the book was released in 1970, featuring Pat Boone as Wilkerson and Erik Estrada as Nicky Cruz, it was a box office success and eventually was translated into thirty other languages.

David Wilkerson's ministry expanded over the next decades as he traveled widely, speaking and writing some fifty books. In 1987, he turned his focus again to New York City, working with his brother Don to plant Times Square Church in a theater just off Broadway. His serious tone, however, never changed. "While some have felt his preaching to be often prophetic in its emotional honesty and biblical ethic," wrote one observer in *Christianity Today*, "others have branded him instead as irrelevant, behind the times, or old-fashioned. While Wilkerson consistently preached hard against sin, that is arguable because he saw firsthand the toll sin could take on a life. Countless faces of helpless lives and the cries of hardened addicts perhaps kindled an anger of sorts . . . toward the enemy of our souls."[6]

Nicky Cruz called his mentor "a straight shooter . . . who never danced around anything."[7] The man didn't coddle, he didn't rationalize, he didn't soft-pedal the need for radical conversion, holy living and Holy Spirit power. Only these, he believed, would set men and women free from every evil trap.

35

Jamie Buckingham
(1932–1992)

The Storyteller

He never set out in life to write bestselling books, either on his own or with famous personalities. And certainly not charismatics.

He grew up in a good every-Sunday Southern Baptist family on the Florida coast. Between his junior and senior years at historic Mercer University, he firmed up his personal commitment to Christ at a summer conference center in upstate New York (clearly cessationist, by the way). After graduation, he headed to Southwestern Baptist Theological Seminary (Fort Worth, Texas) to earn two graduate degrees. By then, he and his wife, Jackie, were starting to build their family that would eventually number five children.

His first pastorate at South Main Street Baptist Church, Greenwood, South Carolina, went well for eight years—until it was sabotaged by the sudden exposure of his adulterous affair.

He and his family fled to Harbor City Baptist Church in Melbourne, Florida, keeping quiet about what had happened—but lasted there only fifteen months until the humiliating news from the first church chased him down and triggered a second firing. He was only 35 years old.

As he wallowed in despair, Jamie Buckingham's life lay in ruins. His pastoral ministry was obviously wrecked. Now what?

> Someone, perhaps my mother, had entered a subscription in my name for *Guideposts* magazine. I seldom read *Guideposts,* but in my idle time, which I now had in abundance, I picked it up. Someplace in that particular issue I found a half-page announcement of a writers' workshop to be sponsored by the magazine. The stipulations were simple. Submit a first-person manuscript of 1,500 words following the basic *Guideposts* style. This would be evaluated and judged by an editorial committee who would then pick the best 20 manuscripts. Those selected would receive an all-expenses-paid trip to New York and would attend a one-week writers' workshop, conducted by the magazine editors.[1]

He put together a piece about an Air Force pilot he knew who had survived a midair explosion. Some weeks after sending it in, he was shocked to be informed that he was one of the chosen twenty out of more than two thousand submissions. It was at that workshop that he met John and Elizabeth Sherrill, who mentioned something about helping a former gang leader named Nicky Cruz put his testimony into a book. By week's end, Buckingham had signed a publisher's contract to develop what became the well-known *Run, Baby, Run.*

The process of researching the book plunged him into new understandings of the Holy Spirit's work, which Nicky Cruz had absorbed during his transformation at Teen Challenge.

Within four months, Buckingham found himself at a Full Gospel Business Men's convention in Washington, where he responded to an invitation and was filled with the Spirit . . .

> . . . whom, up until that time, I only recognized as a boring phrase in the Doxology. Almost everything about me was revolutionized—instantly. . . . Everything within me had been striving against God. Like Jacob at Peniel, I had been vainly wrestling with the angel of the Lord trying to have my own way, yet at the same time unwilling to turn loose until he blessed me. Now the blessing had come. And with it, a limp. Yet even the limp—and the scars—are badges of His glory.[2]

The success of *Run, Baby, Run* (more than twelve million sold since its debut in 1968) led to other chances to collaborate with people who needed help crafting their stories. Among the most notable titles were:

- *Shout It from the Housetops* with CBN leader Pat Robertson (1972),
- *Tramp for the Lord* with beloved World War II survivor Corrie ten Boom (1974), and
- *God Can Do It Again* and eight other titles with evangelist Kathryn Kuhlman—plus a biography of her released after her death, *Daughter of Destiny* (1976).

Buckingham did not jump at every writing opportunity, however. He knew that some public figures needed more seasoning before bringing out a book. In his whimsical way, he wrote that big-name preachers needed to be "wise enough to realize that bread taken too soon from the oven always falls. . . . A ministry should first obtain credibility. The book should follow. . . . I know from personal experience that nothing is more exasperating than trying to help a man crank a car which has no gas."[3]

This wise perspective served his readers well during his long tenure as a columnist for *Charisma* magazine. When a sister publication was launched in 1983 entitled *Ministry Today*, Buckingham was the natural choice for senior editor. He was never one to lecture or pontificate; he made his points more often through winsome stories about real people's foibles, including his own. Readers would smile as they absorbed valuable insights.

His book output eventually totaled 22 solo titles and 24 collaborations. In addition, his curiosity about the Holy Land resulted in a video series he anchored that garnered wide distribution.

To his surprise, even his role as a pastor was resurrected at the nondenominational Tabernacle Church he opened in Melbourne, Florida, growing to a membership of four thousand. More than a few fallen clergy found their way to Jamie and Jackie's door over the years, weeping over their sin and wondering how to find forgiveness. The Buckinghams gave loving but clear-eyed counsel from the Scriptures that they themselves had learned the hard way.

Perhaps his kindly, self-deprecating personality shows best in this admission:

> Perfection still eludes me. I am still vulnerable. But most important, I am no longer satisfied with my imperfection. Nor, thank God, am I intimidated by it. I have reached the point of recognizing that God uses imperfect, immoral, dishonest people. In fact, that's all there are these days. All the holy men seem to have gone off and died. There's no one left but us sinners to carry on the ministry.[4]

36

Jack Hayford
(1934–)

On the Way to Majesty

So, just how did a fading, forty-year-old Foursquare church in Van Nuys, California, rise from eighteen remaining members and a part-time pastor in early 1969 to more than 4,300 on an average Sunday only thirteen years later? Was it the rebranding as "The Church on the Way" (a reference to its location on a busy thoroughfare called Sherman Way)? Did the church suddenly come into a seven-figure endowment? Was it the genius of Pastor Jack Hayford?

None of the above. In fact, Hayford had originally intended to stay only briefly, while he continued his main work as dean of students and instructor at the denomination's Bible college. Nevertheless, at about the eight-month mark, he received in his mind what he felt was a divine directive: *You are to stay at this church.* He was not exactly thrilled.

Frankly, I was afraid. Although there had been a good beginning, I feared a permanent assignment to this little congregation. It might mean personal obscurity—pastoring a small Pentecostal church swallowed up in the megalopolis of southern California. Pride and fear I had never recognized now surfaced and had to be confronted.[1]

He ended up staying a full three decades, emphasizing his beliefs that a church should be people-centered, not pastor-centered, and that genuine worship laid the foundation for all other good things. Every Saturday night, he would go through his empty sanctuary laying hands on every seat, asking God to touch whoever would sit there the next morning. He wrote songs to usher people toward the King of kings (the most notable being "Majesty," eventually published in more than two dozen hymnals).

As a result, The Church on the Way grew into a flagship ministry with both English and Spanish congregations, strong missions involvement, intentionally guided prayer meetings, vibrant youth work and a major influence on spiritual renewal across the nation. Sunday mornings seemed to attract everyone from Hollywood elites to the urban poor. Multiple millions of audio and video recordings of Hayford's messages went out.

But he insisted:

We have done nothing to promote, produce or program this growth. Everything we do that might be called a "program" is simply a response to what God has done and is doing. We do our best to keep pace with *His* work—not try to get Him to endorse ours.[2]

The pastor's openness to what God was doing across denominational lines began to be noticed. In 1989, he was a plenary speaker at the Lausanne II Congress on World Evangelization in Manila, the only such Pentecostal, where he spoke on "Passion for Fullness." When the Promise Keepers movement caught fire a few years later, he was often one of its stadium headliners. He emceed the organization's 1997 "Stand in the Gap" rally that filled Washington's National Mall. C-SPAN carried the event live. He co-chaired Billy Graham's 2004 Crusade in the Rose Bowl.

Through all the attention, however, his theology has never wavered—nor been hidden in the shadows. He has consistently made Spirit empowerment one of his cornerstones, using palatable explanations. When a major evangelical publisher invited him to write a book on glossolalia, he chose to title it *The Beauty of Spiritual Language* (as opposed to, say, "the ecstasy of speaking in tongues"). He took two hundred pages to show that this was more than "the domain of either the brainless or emotionally overwrought,"[3] told his own personal story, gave practical instruction and concluded:

> In short, I believe God wants you, me—every Christian—to know that this blessed benefit comes without sectarian requirements or doctrinaire qualifications. The only requirement is that, within our faith in Christ, we express our hunger and thirst for more of God's grace, that we welcome the Holy Spirit to satisfy our quest and then openly receive this resource promised within His Kingdom joys.[4]

Eventually in 2005, as Hayford edged into his seventies, the respected evangelical magazine *Christianity Today* put him on its cover, calling him "The Pentecostal Gold Standard." The six-page feature article (written by senior writer Tim Stafford, a Presbyterian) reported how he has brought Pentecostals and others together "less through grand strategy than by patient outreach, one person at a time. . . . He is, in fact, aggressive about his beliefs, though he presents them graciously, in a way that explains and persuades." It quoted former US Senate chaplain Lloyd Ogilvie as saying, "What an outstanding intellectual Jack is. He is a deeply rooted scholar in the biblical tradition."

And yet, he told the interviewer, "I have a passion to move every Christian to the free exercise of tongues—not as a proof of spirituality but as a privilege for worship and intercession."[5]

His steady hand was called upon in at least two crises: the sudden death of his successor (and son-in-law) Scott Bauer from a brain aneurysm that burst at the end of a 2003 Wednesday night prayer meeting, when he was just 49. Hayford returned to his previous pulpit for a season until a new senior pastor could be installed. That same year, he answered the Foursquare denomination's call to lead it back from a fifteen-million-dollar loss in a phony investment scheme, becoming president for a four-year term.

Today, his influence lives on through his many books, the *Spirit-Filled Life Study Bible*, for which he was the general editor, and The King's University. He founded this seminary just up Sherman Way from his church in Van Nuys, using a large building purchased from a Baptist congregation intending to move. Fifteen years later, the school relocated to the Dallas area under the oversight of Gateway Church, with Hayford remaining involved as chancellor emeritus during his retirement.

But to many, he will always be simply "Pastor Jack," the tall, ever-kind, trustworthy shepherd guiding others *on the way* to a closer connection with the King.

37

Bill Hamon
(1934–)

A Man of Many "Words"

Some charismatics wax enthusiastic about Bill Hamon, calling him a pioneer, the "father of the prophetic movement," even honoring him with appellations such as "Bishop" and "Doctor." Others hear his bold words about prophecy in the current setting, especially personal "words," and ask lots of questions.

What fans and skeptics alike have to acknowledge is that this genial Oklahoman has, over the course of his more than half century of ministry, raised a fair question: Are there actual prophets today who speak for God? To put it another way, when the apostle Paul wrote that "Christ himself gave the apostles, the prophets, the evangelists, the pastors and teachers, to equip his people for works of service, so that the body of Christ may be built up" (Ephesians 4:11), was he making a statement just for the first century or for all time? Modern Christians of all stripes certainly recognize the validity of "pastors and teachers," and generally "evangelists" as well. But what about the first two in the list? Are they still around?

Hamon answers yes without hesitation.

In saying this, he is not just talking about the basic spiritual gift (Greek: *charisma*) of prophecy for a congregation's general "strengthening, encouraging and comfort" (1 Corinthians 14:3) to be channeled through any believer—male or female, ordained or not.[1] He is talking about a specific, set-apart class of seers, a "'Company of Prophets' that God is raising up in these last days . . . to be restored fully to a recognized and active role in the Church. . . . After pioneering the restoration of prophets for over three decades, I can confirm that prophets are accepted in a large portion of the Body of Christ, and there are thousands of prophets around the world."[2] He tags the 1980s as "designated in the counsels of God as the time for the calling forth of the prophet ministry."[3]

Biblical prototypes are not hard to find, of course, especially throughout the Old Testament: Moses confronting Pharaoh, Nathan confronting the adulterous King David, Elisha conveying God's words to everyone from the Shunammite woman to the Gentile commander Naaman, the many writing prophets from Isaiah to Malachi. In the New Testament, we quickly meet the aged Simeon in the Temple, informing Mary what lies ahead for her newborn baby as well as herself . . . John the Baptist heralding the Lamb of God among the crowd at the riverbank . . . and then the greatest Prophet of all, Jesus Christ, who speaks frequently on behalf of His Father throughout the four gospels.

Thereafter, prophets show up a few times in the life of the early church. A group of them in Antioch—what Hamon would

200

call a "prophetic presbytery"—are used by the Spirit to commission Barnabas and Saul/Paul for their first missionary journey (Acts 13:1–2). Several chapters later, we meet "Judas and Silas, who themselves were prophets" (Acts 15:32). A man named Agabus appears briefly twice: once to alert the Antioch church about a coming famine (Acts 11:27–29), the other time to warn Paul that the Jewish leaders in Jerusalem are going to bind him and "will hand him over to the Gentiles" (21:10–11). Agabus was generally accurate, although not entirely: It was actually the Roman commander's troops who extracted Paul from an agitated Jewish mob bent on lynching him themselves.

Across Bill Hamon's fourteen books, he relates dozens of cases of individualized prophecies. For example, a businessman tells:

My wife and I were at a meeting in Sacramento, California, in January, 1973. I was sitting on the platform and my wife was sitting in the audience. Dr. Hamon was prophesying to different individuals under a strong anointing. He pointed to my wife in the audience and then to me on the platform, and asked if we belonged to each other. We said yes, and he called us to him and gave us a prophecy.

The prophecy included statements that God had called us to the ministry and that within one year we would be in another country preaching the Gospel. I did not relate to that, nor did I believe it could be God. But 11 months later God called us to be missionaries in Mexico. At the writing of this testimony we have now been ministering in Mexico for eight years.[4]

Another situation:

I was once prophesying over a church group at a family camp in Prescott, Arizona. A couple was there with a singing group from Utah. I prophesied over them that God was giving them the desires of their heart and answering their prayers for children. Nine months later a child was born to them. They testified later that they had been trying for seven years to have children and were unable to do so. When I visited their church some time later the grandmother of the young mother told me how she had interceded for her granddaughter to have children for seven years. The whole church had been praying as well, because they were prominent in leadership and known by everyone.[5]

This kind of activity has become a hallmark of Bill Hamon's meetings, to the point that he will prophesy over long lines of individuals for hours at a time. Now in his mid-eighties, he freely says he has given personalized words of prophecy to an eye-popping fifty thousand people over the course of his ministry—and has trained another quarter million others to do the same through his Christian International Ministries Network. The Florida-based organization's stated purpose: "To present and promote the cutting edge of what God is doing and saying in the Church."[6]

Hamon does not claim that every prophecy of his or any other prophet is guaranteed to be 100 percent accurate; in his books, he writes openly about what can cause distortion. Nevertheless, he is convinced enough of the value of prophecies to require that all of his be recorded, transcribed into text format and then disseminated for reflection thereafter. He bases this on Paul's admonition to young Timothy regarding "the prophecies once made about you, so that by recalling them you may fight the battle well" (1 Timothy 1:18).

Some question whether these written transcriptions can over time take on the authority of a secondary Scripture, in competition with the Bible. Hamon clearly does not intend this. "The Bible is the highest authority and has the final say in all matters," he writes, going on to tell about a certain minister who claimed that some "word" from the Lord had given him permission to leave his uncooperative wife. Hamon sharply rebuked him, based on Scripture.[7]

His fellow charismatics have written from time to time, however, to advise discernment on the part of Christians; for example, popular author and seminar speaker John Bevere wrote a book with the provocative title and subtitle *Thus Saith the Lord? How to know when God is speaking to you through another*. It was released by Creation House, a well-known charismatic publisher.

The eminent theologian Wayne Grudem, for some years the Association of Vineyard Churches' guiding light on doctrinal matters, warns, "People who continually seek subjective 'messages' from God to guide their lives must be cautioned that subjective personal guidance is not a primary function of New Testament prophecy. . . . Many charismatic writers would agree with this caution." He goes on to cite three of them: Michael Harper (see chapter 33), Donald Gee (see chapter 10) and another British pastor/author named Donald Bridge.[8]

No one could ever accuse Bill Hamon of seeking to control those who come for his ministry, of manipulating them or of trying to fleece them financially. His motives are clean. He makes no attempt to rebut his critics; he just continues to do what he believes God has called him to do.

In light of his overall track record, perhaps the best course of action for Christians today is what Paul advised two different churches under his care:

"Two or three prophets should speak, and the others should weigh carefully what is said" (1 Corinthians 14:29).

"Do not quench the Spirit. Do not treat prophecies with contempt but test them all; hold on to what is good" (1 Thessalonians 5:19–20).

38

John Wimber
(1934–1997)

In the "Radical Middle"

Sunday after Sunday, the pastor and his wife drove home discouraged, even frustrated. He had kept up his sermon series from the gospel of Luke, where healing stories (some two dozen) were unavoidable. And Jesus had not done all the healing Himself; sometimes it was the Twelve, or even the Seventy-Two. Every Sunday at the end of the service, John Wimber invited those needing prayer to stay behind for the laying on of hands. The results so far: Nothing. Zero.

After a particularly fruitless Sunday, his phone rang early the next morning. One of his newer members said he had just gotten a new job and *had* to go to work that day, despite the fact that his wife was sick with a fever. "I can't stay home and take care of the kids, and we can't find a babysitter. Can you come pray for her?"

The pastor could hardly say no. But after hanging up the phone, he stared at the ceiling. "God," he said, "look what You've got me into this time. This guy really believes this stuff. He's going to lose his job, or I'm going to have to take care of his kids today."

When I arrived at the house the husband led me into their bedroom. Her face was red and swollen with fever. *Oh, no,* I groaned inwardly, *this looks like a hard one.* I walked over and laid hands on her, mumbled a faithless prayer, and then I turned around and began explaining to her husband why some people do not get healed—a talk I had perfected during the previous ten months. I was well into my explanation when his eye caught something behind me. Then he started grinning. I turned around to see his wife out of bed, looking like a new person. "What's happened to you?" I asked.

"I'm well," she said. "You healed me. Would you like to stay for some coffee and breakfast?"

I could not believe it. She was well. I politely declined her offer of hospitality and left. Halfway back to my car, I fully realized what had happened. All the months of questioning and despair, excitement and disappointment, revelation and humiliation—the full force of these emotions and hopes washed over me. Then I became euphoric and giddy. And I yelled at the top of my lungs, "We got one!"[1]

That breakthrough in February 1978 was the launch for the next two decades of healing and renewal ministry not only in Wimber's congregation (eventually named Vineyard Christian Fellowship of Anaheim) but across a wide array of churches and even into the classrooms of Pasadena's prestigious Fuller Theological Seminary. He often pointed out that 38.5 percent of the four gospels' narrative verses (484 out of 1,257) describe

Jesus' miracles, and that He had commissioned His followers to do even greater things than He had found time to do while on earth. Wimber said this did not need to be limited to special crusades or settings; it was entirely fitting for the local church scene.

None of this understanding had come naturally to him. He had been raised in a nonreligious home, grew up to excel as a jazz musician and had come to Christ only at age 29 through the influence of his drummer's home Bible study. He then enrolled in Azusa Pacific College (now University) to earn a degree in biblical studies and joined the staff of a Friends (Quaker) church in Yorba Linda. If anything, the culture here was pietistic, quiet, controlled. In 1974, Fuller asked him to head up a new Department of Church Growth.

> I wanted no part of being "charismatic." As a church consultant, I had dealt constantly with schisms across the country wrought by so-called charismatics. So when God began dealing with me, I was very afraid of embarrassing myself, losing friends, constituents, and colleagues.
>
> Most of the healing models I'd seen were totally foreign to me. I'd been to tent meetings on three occasions and also watched television, and it was so theatrical and flamboyant. . . . There were also questions about integrity, financial abuse, extravagant claims, self-aggrandizing attitudes—it was frightening to me, not appetizing at all.
>
> But I couldn't escape the fact that God did heal through Jesus, and I'd been called to be one of his disciples. I couldn't dismiss that.[2]

His experiences doing personal evangelism and leading Bible studies eventually led him back to the pastorate. More Vineyard congregations sprang up under his leadership. He suggested to his colleague at Fuller, Dr. C. Peter Wagner, that they might collaborate on a course to explore the miraculous and its connection to evangelism. After getting faculty approval, MC 510 was launched on a Monday night in the fall of 1982 under the title "Signs, Wonders and Church Growth." Wimber did most of the three-hour lectures while Wagner watched approvingly. At the end of each session, students were invited to practice what they had just heard, laying hands on one another for healing.

The undeniable results—and the surrounding publicity—catapulted both men into the national spotlight. A faculty panel convened to evaluate whether this belonged in a seminary curriculum or not. Magazines ran cover stories. Wimber declined to be pigeonholed as Pentecostal or charismatic; he preferred to be pegged as somewhere in the "radical middle" of Christianity.[3] He never claimed that God would always heal in answer to believing prayer. But that did not dissuade him from continuing to ask. In his 1987 book, *Power Healing*, he wrote:

> I am convinced that sometimes Christians' demands for exhaustive knowledge are excuses for not believing in and acting on what they know. . . . While acknowledging that I will never exhaustively understand divine healing, I am satisfied to act on what I know now, confident that I will know more fully in the future. To paraphrase Blaise Pascal, "I believe, therefore I will know . . . eventually."[4]

When *Christianity Today* invited him to a panel on "Wonder-working Power," he told about speaking in Melbourne, Australia, when the Lord had impressed him with a word of knowledge for a certain woman in the audience who had undergone two less-than-helpful surgeries to resolve her cleft palate. He told her that God would heal her.

A Christian surgeon became very concerned. He said, "Do you understand what you've promised that woman?" . . . He explained rather ardently for ten minutes the nature of bones and how the cranium was a bone and that the inside of the mouth was a bone. "Do you understand what a mature bone is like?" he said. "You have to surgically break that bone in order for this palate to come together."

And I said, "All I can tell you is what God told me, and I believe that if you'll go join the prayer group you'll watch this woman get healed." He just looked at me as if I had six heads!

Three days later the woman's palate closed. So the surgeon hurried her off to his offices and examined her, giving us one of those miracles that is authenticated.[5]

As the Vineyard network kept expanding to more than five hundred churches,[6] John Wimber had a lot to manage. A sizable test came in the early 1990s, when revival broke out at the Toronto Airport Vineyard, with nightly meetings full of healings, prophecies, deliverances—and controversial manifestations (shaking, falling down, laughter, even roaring). Wimber kept a level bearing for a while, noting that similar things had taken place in awakenings throughout church history. "Most people love babies, but they don't necessarily like the details of the birthing process. The birthing of a child is a messy experience at best. . . . The same thing applies to revival. . . .

"In my opinion, it's not necessary to explain everything connected with revival any more than a young mother needs to share in detail the travail of the birthing process. All she has to do is hold that baby up, and everyone shares in the joy."[7]

Eventually, however, he came to feel that the Toronto displays were dominating the attention and withdrew the Vineyard endorsement. The church renamed itself and continues to this day.

A parallel issue arose the next year in Kansas City, where a group of prophets were espousing questionable doctrines. Wimber and the Vineyard attempted to bring counsel and guidance for a while, but eventually the Kansas City group chose to disengage.

None of these things deterred John Wimber, however, from seeking the open, sincere flow of the power of God—not for its own sake, but for its value in advancing God's Kingdom. Perhaps his heart shows best in this observation from late in his life: "God doesn't revive people who have it all together. He revives people who are hungry, thirsty, weak, naked, blind, and less than spotless."[8]

39

Jane Hansen Hoyt
(1936–)

Out from Behind the Mask

Pastor's daughters learn early to guard their public image. The congregation is always watching, and so a wholesome, modest, pleasant persona works best for all concerned. Little Jane was no different, despite the tensions rippling through her life at home.

Her father was successful as both a preacher and a musician . . . too busy, in fact, to give her more than a hurried hug on his way out the door. Her mother kept a proper home while wishing for more emotional support. Then, when Jane was eleven, a marital crisis erupted over her dad's too-friendly relationship with a flattering woman in the church. Her mother caught on to what was brewing, felt all the more insecure and turned to her daughter for solace.

I hated this emotional battleground. I was caught in the middle, waving a small white handkerchief of truce in every direction, but nobody seemed to notice. . . .

I wanted desperately for all the hurt and anger to go away forever. I felt responsible, as if I were the only stable one in the storm. What I wanted was a family, but I couldn't fix all their problems.

One day [shortly before her thirteenth birthday], alone on my bed, I made a quiet decision, not realizing at that young age that it was actually a vow. The results of that vow affected me emotionally for years.

I swore to myself that no man would ever hurt me the way Dad hurt my mother.[1]

The marriage eventually recovered—enough that when Jane herself was eighteen and a nice-looking young man with a ready smile at church started paying attention to her, she quickly said yes to his proposal. A baby son came along. But things were happening too fast, with not enough preparation. By age twenty, Jane was single again, more distressed than ever.

It would be another three years before she regained enough composure to marry Howard Hansen, a pastor's son with a reliable job in the travel industry. While their relationship seemed lukewarm at times, it was at least stable. A daughter and then another son were born, and the family settled into a local Lutheran church. Jane helped with vacation Bible school and got into a circle of supportive women.

By then it was the late 1960s, with spiritual renewal springing up in mainline denominations. Living in the Seattle area, she heard about a women's group called Aglow that was just taking shape. The name had come from a certain translation of Romans 12:10–11, "Be devoted to one another . . . never lagging behind in diligence; aglow in the Spirit, *enthusiastically* serving the Lord" (AMP).

She read Fr. Dennis Bennett's book *Nine O'Clock in the Morning* (see chapter 20) and learned more about the Holy Spirit's work. Could this maybe help her inner discomfort?

> I knew I had to get myself to the Friday night meeting at St. Luke's where Dennis Bennett talked about the baptism in the Holy Spirit. It was an appointment I needed to keep. I drove with a friend to the Ballard district, and we walked into St. Luke's, where we sat in the very back of the church.
>
> I listened closely as Father Bennett talked about how the Holy Spirit was poured out at Pentecost. He not only described the events Luke recorded in the book of Acts, but he shared his own experience of being filled with the Holy Spirit and receiving the gift of tongues.
>
> I'd never heard anything like what happened next. A man named Stanley gave a "message in tongues." It was beautiful, rhythmical, like someone speaking in another language.
>
> Silence hung in the room for a few minutes. Then, a gray-haired lady named Edna stepped forward, faced the audience and gave the interpretation in English, speaking in the exact rhythmic pattern Stanley had spoken in.
>
> This was the Holy Spirit. I knew it in the deepest part of my being. All my reservations dissolved.[2]

By the end of the meeting, Jane Hansen was at the altar wanting to be prayed for. Her walk in Spirit empowerment began that night. When she spoke in tongues herself a few weeks later in her bedroom, "the heavens opened as I'd never experienced, bathing me in waves of the Father's love. . . . My heart flooded over with the deep realization of being accepted, loved and forgiven. I didn't want to leave the room."[3]

Her contact with the Aglow women kept deepening, as did her relationship with her husband over a period of time. Harmony settled into the marriage. At the local Aglow chapter, she was surprised to be asked to lead it; more than a hundred women showed up for the first luncheon meeting she and her team arranged. One thing led to another over the coming years, until finally in 1980 she was elected president of the whole Aglow organization.

But first, her liberation from inner qualms had to become complete. If she were to lead other women into freedom in the Spirit, she needed to know its fullness herself. At the end of a conference in Penticton, British Colombia, Pastor Jack Hayford (see chapter 36) approached her quietly and said, "I feel I need to pray for you before you leave."

> He knelt beside my chair, praying quietly in the Spirit. "I feel that the Lord is telling me to peel a mask off of your face," he said to me. I felt him touch my cheek as he began the motion of peeling off a covering over my countenance. He began at the chin, then up over my cheeks, my eyes and finally over my forehead.
>
> At the time, I knew something profound was happening. This man of God, under guidance of the Holy Spirit, foreshadowed perfectly what the Lord would do in me during the next few years.
>
> The façade that covered my face was being peeled off in preparation for a new work of God.[4]

If you watch Jane today at the helm of Aglow International, you will not sense any hiding behind a mask of insecurity or hesitation. She boldly leads a ministry of more than three thousand local clusters (called "Lighthouses") across 170 nations—

having traveled to many of them. The organization has evolved over the decades, encouraging gender reconciliation (female-male), doing outreaches to the poor, going into women's prisons and safe houses and in recent years enthusiastically supporting the nation of Israel.

Along the way, she weathered the personal loss of her beloved Howard. She subsequently married a retired gentleman named Tony Hoyt, who encourages her in her present calling. She has a particular talent, says her current pastor, for making people feel loved and for recognizing their latent gifts. Though now in her mid-eighties, she remains determined that God's purposes for His daughters will not be sidelined.

40

David Mainse

(1936–2017)

At Canada's Crossroads

In the spring of 1962, Pembroke, Ontario, had just gotten its first television station (black-and-white, of course). That sparked an idea in the mind of a local 25-year-old Pentecostal[1] pastor, who was just then booking services for his brothers-in-law, a quartet. What if they could sing for just fifteen minutes after the late news on Saturday night?

He approached the owner, made his pitch and got a somewhat gruff reply: "Okay, David—but no preaching! All you can do is introduce the music."

So that is what happened on June 2. The cost: $55, which was slightly more than twice the pastor's weekly salary. By the next Wednesday, the owner was calling back in a friendlier mood to say, "I've had more letters and phone calls about your program than in the six months we've been on the air. Anytime you have good music like that, you can come back."

David Mainse smiled as he replied, "I'll be back this week!"[2]

And so was born his foray into mass media, never imagining how central it would become in his future. He called the little program *Crossroads* (joking years later that maybe he should have chosen *Saturday Night Live* instead). The format was set from the start; instead of preaching, he would use music (sometimes by his soloist wife, Norma Jean) and interviews to engage viewers in a low-key, comfortable experience. His trademark question for guests became "So, how has God worked in your life?"

Gradually, more stations picked up the show and viewership increased, until in 1971 he resigned his pastorate to give full time to television. What better way to span the vastness of the world's second-largest country—especially when the temperature huddles well below zero? Mainse's warm smile and handsome face became a mainstay across many markets, to the point that a new studio was created in rented space in downtown Toronto; its address became the name for the daily hourlong show, *100 Huntley Street*. All of this required sizable fund-raising, of course, which made him nervous. But viewers stepped up to see that the bills were paid.

In the early 1980s, Mainse and his team convinced the government's broadcast regulator to let religious groups own and operate their own stations and even channels—something that had not been allowed for half a century. The guest list for *100 Huntley Street* over the years reads like a who's who of Christendom: street preacher Nicky Cruz, Canadian pioneer missionary to India Mark Buntain, various Catholic charismatic priests, Joni Eareckson Tada, singer Jeremy Camp, the Toronto Blue Jays' Cy Young Award–winning knuckleball pitcher R. A. Dickey, evangelist Billy Graham. Just as important in Mainse's mind, however, was the bank of phone counselors, where real-time dialogue and prayer still take place even during the show. Some thirty thousand calls are received each month.

Today, it is Canada's longest-running daily show on television. It pulls in 1.3 million viewers a week; only two other programs do better (*Hockey Night in Canada* and the Canadian Football League games). Headquartered now in its own 143,000-square-foot complex down the lakeshore in Burlington, Ontario, the umbrella entity called Crossroads Christian Communications produces auxiliary shows in nineteen languages for everyone from children to married couples to Canada's First Nation peoples.

But during his lifetime, Mainse's impact ranged beyond the world of television. One example among many: the eye-catching Pavilion of Promise he spearheaded in the middle of Vancouver's Expo '86 fair. Its three connected theaters drew thousands of visitors daily from June through mid-October to see multimedia presentations of the Gospel story. Even before Opening Day, he had to deal with opposition from an "interfaith" group that opposed the idea of an exclusively Christian exhibit. The supreme court of the province finally settled the matter by noting that the complainants had never applied for their own pavilion, thus clearing the way.

"That struggle gave us a million dollars of publicity," said Mainse afterward. "Now that we're open, that's the reason we have such long lines. I'd like to thank the interfaith group."[3]

Vancouver was said, in fact, to be the *least* churchgoing city in North America. The city's main newspaper grumbled about Pavilion of Promise's "violence" (referring to the crucifixion scene). But a local counterculture paper called it "visually impressive." One Los Angeles daily listed it first on its "big winners" list.

And more important than any accolades, the endeavor brought hundreds of fairgoers to make first-time decisions to follow Christ. As a result, Crossroads continued to exhibit at several more world's fairs across the globe. No wonder the Empowered21 leadership network gave David Mainse a Lifetime Global Impact Award in 2015 for "significant impact on the world through the power of the Holy Spirit."

His gracious manner and clean reputation earned him plaudits from two prime ministers of opposing parties: Pierre Trudeau (Liberal) and Brian Mulroney (Progressive Conservative). After he passed away in September 2017 (from MDS leukemia), the *Globe and Mail* (Canada's newspaper of record) called him a "genial soul."[4]

Perhaps California pastor/blogger Karl Vaters said it best when he posted, "I want to be like David Mainse when I grow up. . . . David was as far removed from the televangelist stereotype as a person could be. Always gentle, modest and humble—even comically naïve at times—David always seemed like the last person who would want the spotlight. But he found himself in that position because his greatest passion was to worship Jesus and share Christ's love with others. And he did so by using whatever technology would allow him to reach the greatest number of people possible."[5]

41

Jesse Miranda
(1937–2019)

Up from the Barrio

Little Jesse was just six years old when he first climbed up into the Albuquerque church bus to ride to Sunday school. There he learned many things, including how to write. They gave him toys for Christmas. They spoke about a Jesus who loved Mexican-Americans like him, would save them, and would even heal them.

His parents said little about all this; after all, his father—a sawmill worker who had received less than one month of schooling—claimed to be Catholic, while his mother—who had gotten as far as third grade—was only a nominal Protestant. But when Jesse was eight, she became seriously ill. Her young son told the people at his little church about this, and soon they showed up at the Miranda home to pray for her. She recovered.

Moving into his early teens, the boy thought much about spiritual things. One day he said, "Dad, Catholics never read the Bible," because he had never seen him read it. "Mother, you read the Bible," he continued, "but you never come to the book of Acts."

> And then they would turn around and say, "And you Pentecostals never *leave* the book of Acts." So I saw my shortcomings and I saw differences. Yet we loved and respected one another. . . . We all affirmed one another.[1]

Growing up in the *barrio*, Jesse avoided the pervasive gangs and drugs. He and his friends chose rather to hang out in one of the many junk cars and use their imaginations.

> We'd sit in the cars and say, "Let's go to California"—wherever that was. One would say, "I see the mountains," then "I see the desert." Finally somebody'd say, "I see the ocean—I guess we got there."[2]

The fantasy became reality after high school, when Jesse Miranda managed to enroll at the Assemblies of God's Southern California Bible College (now Vanguard University), where he would earn a bachelor's degree. Along the way, his hometown pastor back in New Mexico nudged him one summer to start a church in a storefront, despite a bar on one side and a dance hall on the other. He made it work. The Assemblies ordained him by the age of twenty, he married a young woman named Susan, and they began ministry in the Hispanic churches of the Southwest. In just a couple of years, Latin American Bible Institute invited him to teach courses.

While gradually taking on more and more denominational responsibilities, he somehow found time and energy over the years to earn two master's degrees (one at the Christian institution Biola University, the other at Cal State–Fullerton) and even a doctorate at Fuller Theological Seminary. That may have been the fruit of his mother's long-ago comment after pointing out "the only man I ever knew, until I was probably twenty years old, that had a degree. Joe Martinez was there, and he was at the altar on his knees, and he was a layman but a university professor." Said Mrs. Miranda, "Now, son, I'd like for you to be an educated man."[3] The image made a permanent impression.

Always a keen listener, his exposure to the wider Christian landscape led him to notice two concerns. One was that many Hispanic church leaders seemed disconnected from each other. By 1992, he had founded the *Alianza de Ministerios Evangelicos Nacionales* (abbreviated *AMEN*) to encourage interaction. (Nine years later, the network merged into today's National Hispanic Christian Leadership Conference—NHCLC—which embraces more than forty thousand congregations.)

The second, even wider, problem was absence from the majority Christian power centers.

> I was watching a cable television station that was carrying a meeting of evangelicals on racial reconciliation. I was excited to see this demonstration of Christian unity. But then my phone rang, and a Hispanic leader on the other end asked if I was watching this. When I told him I was, he asked, "Is your TV in black and white? Because mine is; it looks like a rerun from the 1960s. Why aren't we part of this discussion?"[4]

Miranda bore no grudge against African-American Christians; he sought only to get into the dialogue alongside them, to "help us all work through the differences of skin pigmentation, culture, or history."[5] He believed there was value to be gained from ethnic Americans who "live in the hyphen." He called upon Christians of all hues to highlight not only the Exodus story (deliverance from oppression), but also the Samaritan story of John 4, where Jesus engaged someone nearby from a different ethnicity. In a *Christianity Today* commentary, he wrote:

> The Samaritans, being both Jew and Gentile, were the half-breeds or *mestizos* of the time. Despite strong historical, cultural, and religious taboos, Jesus speaks with the woman. His disciples, carriers of the dominant Jewish tradition, are numbed, indifferent and both literally and figuratively "out to lunch" during this prophetic encounter. Meanwhile, Jesus affirms the woman's personhood and leads her to faith in him. She, in turn, spreads the good news of the Gospel to her community, creating a new cultural and spiritual paradigm. . . .
>
> Under the skin, we are all kin. We are all members of the human race and *familia*.[6]

This kind of viewpoint, graciously expressed, opened many doors for Jesse Miranda. Azusa Pacific University, one of the largest evangelical schools, invited him to become its associate dean of urban and ethnic affairs; he served in this role for nearly a decade. Even the White House took notice; three US presidents in a row (George H. W. Bush, Bill Clinton and George W. Bush) sought his counsel on Hispanic affairs.

But he never abandoned his book-of-Acts convictions. At the age of 63, he returned to the college where he had started, Vanguard, to support its Hispanic students and set up a Center for Urban Studies and Ethnic Leadership. "The church was born to be global," he insisted. "The church must not see diversity as a problem to be solved but rather as the way to complete its prophetic identity. To this end, racial and ethnic groups are the social and spiritual capital of the Body of Christ."[7]

When the boy from the *barrio* passed away in 2019, Samuel Rodriguez, his successor at NHCLC (who himself has received White House access), summarized Miranda's life with passion on Facebook: "His commitment to Christ, real. His prophetic voice, renewing. His love for the marginalized, relentless. I love and forever will honor you, Bro. Jesse! You changed my life!"

42

Reinhard Bonnke

(1940–2017)

Plundering Hell to Populate Heaven

I f you were plotting a good career path for a white evangelist, you would most likely advise him to start on friendly
turf with well-heeled donors, such as in America. Once
his media programs and sizable constituency were in place, he
could then begin reaching out to other nations.

Such was not the case with Reinhard Bonnke. His begin-
nings in childhood peril under Hitler's Third Reich (he, with his
mother and siblings, fled to Denmark while his father served in
the *Wehrmacht*) gave no hint that he would someday preach—
in English, not his native German—to massive crowds across
Africa for more than forty years.

Once World War II was over, his father was able to rejoin the
family and soon became a Pentecostal pastor. Young Reinhard
was born again at the age of nine, and not long after sensed

God's call to ministry himself. He experienced the baptism in the Holy Spirit and eventually enrolled at the Bible College of Wales, founded by the renowned intercessor Rees Howells.

Back in Germany, he was ordained, began to preach, and met his future wife, Anni, at a gospel music festival; she impressed him with her gracious handling of a wrongly pitched accompaniment that caused her to lose the singing competition. They married and pastored a small church until 1967, when the burden for Africa grew so strong that they pulled up stakes and headed for Lesotho, a primitive mountain kingdom inside South Africa.

The next seven years in traditional missionary work were not particularly successful. Bonnke was frustrated, and he prayed much about what should change. In 1974, he began having a dream, night after night, in which he saw a map of the whole African continent filled with blood, and the voice of God declaring, "Africa shall be saved!" He took this to mean that the blood of Christ would redeem the souls of men and women on a major scale.

He acquired a modest tent and set it up in Gabarone, the capital of newly independent Botswana, just north of South Africa. The first night, only a hundred people came to hear him preach the Gospel. He was not discouraged; each night the crowd grew, and more people found salvation, until the final meeting filled a ten-thousand-seat stadium.

From that moment on, Bonnke's approach was settled: He would lead evangelistic campaigns wherever possible, to reach as many as possible—black, white and any other race. He set up an entity called Christ for all Nations, CfaN (not to be confused with Gordon Lindsay's CFNI—Christ For The Nations Institute—in America). His boldly stated vision: "Plundering Hell to Populate Heaven."

Three years after the first tent, he bought a much bigger one that would seat ten thousand . . . and in 1983, the largest Gospel tent ever constructed, to hold 34,000. But he didn't get to use it for long. A severe windstorm in Cape Town blew it apart a year later. Not to be deterred, Bonnke opted from then on to take most of his crusades outdoors, in parks and other open spaces, with floodlights, powerful sound systems and eventually large video screens placed around the perimeter. Also provided were barrels to contain bonfires, where newly saved listeners could rid themselves of any magic amulets or charms. Crowds swelled into the hundreds of thousands; some estimates ran past one million on a given night. Press reports started calling him the "Billy Graham of Africa."

Over the years, he campaigned in nearly every one of the continent's 54 nations. He met face-to-face with fourteen different African heads of state, not all of them Christians. He even dared to go into heavily Muslim areas such as northern Nigeria. In 1991, a protest broke out in Kano over rumors that he was planning to "lead an invasion" and would blaspheme Islam. A mob of eight thousand youths rioted after Friday prayers and began attacking Christians as well as burning several churches. With actual lives in jeopardy, Bonnke elected not to continue his meetings—one of the rare times he backed down. But in a few years, he returned to preach again in Nigeria. "A man of faith has no reverse gear," he insisted.

If anyone doubted whether the Jesus he preached was real, they had to reconsider as they watched Bonnke pray for the sick. Blind people came up on the platform to prove they could now see; the lame and deformed demonstrated how they could now run; out in the audience, hundreds of needy people found faith to jump up from wheelchairs. The evangelist truly believed, as he told an American interviewer, that "if we preach what the apostles preached, we will have the results the apostles had."[1]

Would that even include raising the dead, as both Peter and Paul had done? In November 2001, a Nigerian pastor named Daniel Ekechukwu was driving to deliver a Christmas gift to his father when, coming down a steep hill, his brakes suddenly failed. His car slammed into a stone pillar, thrusting his chest into the steering wheel and his head into the windshield. At the hospital, the attending physician filled out a death certificate after finding neither heartbeat nor breath.

In the morgue, his body was embalmed (although, by African custom, his organs were not removed). His distraught wife, however, refused to bury him until she first arranged to have him transported in the casket (three days later) to a nearby church where Bonnke was preaching.

Church officials hesitated to bring the casket into the main service; instead, it was taken to the basement, where the lid was opened. There, while the sermon continued upstairs, Ekechukwu suddenly sat up, opened his eyes, and began to breathe again. The entire episode, with multiple verifications, is recounted in a six-part series of YouTube videos.[2] Let the viewer decide . . .

Yet, healing was never the main point of Bonnke's ministry. It merely served to draw Africans to the healing Savior. "Some people call me a healing evangelist," he complained to *Christianity Today*. "I do not like that. I define myself as a salvation evangelist who also prays for the sick. Wherever we go, 95 percent of the meeting is a clear preaching presentation of the gospel."[3] According to CfaN's tally of his many campaigns, more than 97 million made decisions for Christ—a number based not just on an estimate of raised hands, but on individuals actually filling out information cards.

In the same meetings, untold thousands were baptized in the Holy Spirit. "If the church rejects the Holy Spirit, He is homeless—like the dove Noah sent out from the ark that couldn't land just any place," Bonnke said. "We must always make Him, the heavenly Dove, welcome in our midst."

43

Kevin & Dorothy Ranaghan
(1940–) / (1942–)

Catholic to the Core

Their names and education give you a strong clue: You can't get much more Catholic (even *Irish* Catholic!) than Notre Dame graduates Kevin and Dorothy (Garrity) Ranaghan. Both had earned master's degrees by the time they married in 1966; he later went on to nail down a PhD in liturgical studies (1973). They had not yet reached their first wedding anniversary when friends at another Catholic university in Pittsburgh (Duquesne) started telling them about their fresh, new "baptism in the Holy Spirit." What was this all about, anyway?

"So, my reaction here was pretty negative, and so was Dorothy's," Kevin recalls. He was at this point teaching at Saint Mary's College just across the avenue from Notre Dame, while Dorothy taught at a Catholic high school. "But we knew these people well. I mean, they were solid, responsible, renewal-minded Catholics and they were scholars. We were all students or professors in theology, church history, and philosophy."[1] This plunged him into a six-week personal study of what the Bible actually said about the topic.

Dorothy admits, "We could see that even in their faces there was something changed and different, and so although we wanted to discount what they were saying as sounding a little fringe-y, we could not deny the experience we saw. . . . And whatever it was . . . we came to see we wanted that, too. We wanted more. We didn't even know what the 'more' was sometimes, but we wanted more, more of the Lord, more work to do, and more empowerment."[2]

So, now what? With some of their Notre Dame friends, they reached out to the local Full Gospel Business Men's Fellowship chapter president, Ray Bullard. That resulted in a groundbreaking, if sometimes awkward, Monday night meeting of nine young Catholics and a group of Pentecostal pastors in Bullard's basement. The two sides sparred for a while about whether speaking in tongues was all that necessary theologically. But then the Catholics said they were at least open to the idea. One of them recounted:

> At a certain point, we said we were willing to give it a try, and a man explained to us what was involved. Very late that evening, sometime after midnight, down in that basement room, the brothers lined us up on one side of the room and the ministers on the other side of the room, and they began to pray in tongues and to walk toward us with outstretched hands. Before they reached us, many of us began to pray and sing in tongues.[3]

Kevin immediately sensed a new surge of joy as well as a renewed faith. The words of Scripture seemed to light up. After he went home that night and told Dorothy what had happened, she received her infilling the next day alone in a chapel. "It was like the Lord planted a flag in the center of my life and said, *This is permanent—hang on to this!*"

Soon they started a prayer meeting on the Notre Dame campus that drew up to four hundred people a week. Verbal gifts of the Spirit were welcomed, and when prayer for the sick was offered, healings took place. The first of many annual charismatic conferences on the Notre Dame campus happened that summer, soaring over the next decade to an attendance peak of thirty thousand. The Ranaghans wrote a book, *Catholic Pentecostals,* to chronicle what was going on and how it fit with Catholic theology; Kevin viewed Spirit baptism as "an adult, mature affirmation of Christian initiation. It is everything that Baptism and Confirmation are meant to be. It is a new beginning."[4] Given his and his wife's credentials, Paulist Press was willing to publish the book in 1969 (as well as another title, *As the Spirit Leads Us,* two years later).

Their thoughtful leadership throughout the years did much to explain various church styles to each other. He insisted that the freewheeling practices of American Pentecostalism were cultural, not central. "We have to be very careful," he told *St. Anthony Messenger,* a Franciscan magazine, "to distinguish between what is essential in the experience of the Holy Spirit in the life of the Christian and what is a religious-cultural form of expressing that experience. On the one hand we have to be open enough to have respect for people's traditions where they are. But these are merely peripheral to the Baptism of the Holy Spirit, to the exercise of the fruits and gifts of the Holy Spirit."[5]

Kevin was named executive director of the National Service Committee of the Catholic Charismatic Renewal and led its work for more than a decade. Dorothy also served on this committee and edited its newsletter for seven years. Kevin became known as an able organizer of conferences, including the 1977 multidenominational gathering that filled Kansas City's Arrowhead Stadium with fifty thousand people, half of them Catholics. For this and other similar large gatherings, he knew there would need to be some kind of structure for spiritual utterances, without quenching the Spirit. So, he formed "word gift units" of up to ten carefully vetted persons, who sat in a group near the main podium and had their own microphone to give prophecies, tongues and interpretations.

Kevin Ranaghan has never been a priest, but he was ordained back in 1973 as a deacon of the church, which in Catholic order does not carry a salary. As early as 1971, he and Dorothy helped start an intentional charismatic community in South Bend called the People of Praise, which has been their home ever since. He did not retire from active ministry until April 2019, as he neared his eightieth birthday.

Looking back on the renewal landscape, he observes, "I guess sociologists would say that we [various denominations and groupings] couldn't have gotten along, and yet we were really united in prayer and in the love of Christ. There is a definite ecumenical aspect to this movement. It is creating a lot of understanding on the grassroots level."[6]

44

John & Carol Arnott
(1940–)/(1943–)

Catching Fire in the Frozen North

The bone-chilling deep freeze of January 1994 spread misery across much of North America's eastern side, bursting water pipes, closing schools and causing more than one hundred deaths. On the fifteenth, Toronto's thermometers sank to -26 degrees Celsius (-15 degrees Fahrenheit). On the nineteenth, 67 new record lows were set, from Kentucky to Quebec.

Nevertheless, on the next night, a Thursday, 120 souls braved the frigid elements to show up at their modest strip-mall church, the Toronto Airport Vineyard, where a visiting speaker from St. Louis was to begin a four-night series. Randy Clark preached his message, then invited listeners to come forward for prayer. Then . . . to everyone's surprise, the scene "exploded" (Pastor John Arnott's word) into intense praise, worship and deliverance.

Some cried with relief from long-festering fears and resentments; others rejoiced aloud, to the point of laughing. Some were so overcome by the presence of God that they could only lie on the floor in front of the pulpit.

"It hadn't occurred to us," he wrote, "that God would throw a massive party where people would laugh, roll, cry and become so empowered that emotional hurts from childhood would just lift off."[1] No one quite knew what to think.

But the same thing recurred on Friday night, and then Saturday night. Before Sunday dawned, Arnott was pleading with Clark not to go home just yet. The revival rolled on and on, as meetings continued every night of the week except Mondays. Clark kept ministering into early spring (except for short trips back to his family and congregation at the St. Louis Vineyard).

Word spread, and crowds swelled at the small building. Waiting lines started forming as early as five o'clock for doors that would not open until seven. Healings became common. People started showing up from outside the metro area, then from the United States, even from Europe. One estimate tallied fifty thousand unique visitors in the first six months, leading *Toronto Life* magazine to name the church the year's number-one tourist attraction.

A British newspaper coined the term the "Toronto Blessing," which didn't exactly please the Arnotts; they much preferred the "Father's blessing" instead. London's *Sunday Telegraph* came up with a headline that ran, "British Airways Flight 092 Took Off from Toronto Airport . . . just as the Holy Spirit Was Landing on a Small Church 100 Yards from the End of the Runway."

In November, the church was able to rent a former conference center that seated four thousand, still near the airport. Hotels started running shuttles to assist guests each evening. John Arnott struggled to keep the attention on the Spirit's internal work in human lives instead of what the manifestations looked like. "We are talking about a relationship with the King," he insisted. So, what did people learn from being on the floor? "That God is in control."[2]

A young reporter, Lorna Dueck, showed up to cover the story:

> I was significantly discouraged about Christian ministry at the time. In spite of my angst, I was curious about the bizarre stories of spiritual manifestations. . . . I remember going to the back of the church, phoning my sister, and complaining, "Everyone is getting this 'Father's blessing' here but me." My charismatic sister told me to put down my notepad, stop being a reporter, and just receive. . . .
>
> I ended up attending for a week. . . . On those nights I was prayed for, I spent a few hours of my own in "carpet time," the . . . term for what happens when people are knocked down, "slain in the Spirit," and leave mysteriously strengthened and renewed in their love for God.[3]

Today, a quarter century later, Lorna Dueck is CEO of Crossroads Christian Communications, home of Canada's long-running *100 Huntley Street* television show (see chapter 40).

A sober-minded sociologist, Dr. Margaret Poloma, came from the University of Akron and ended up doing formal research in 1995 on nearly one thousand visitors to the church.

> Nearly 9 out of 10 respondents indicated that they were "more in love with Jesus now than I have ever been in my life," and that they had "come to know the Father's love in new ways." The fresh experience of God's love carried over into relationships, especially marital ones, where 88 percent of married respondents indicated a greater love for their spouses as a result of the

Blessing. . . . A follow-up survey of the original respondents conducted in 1997, two years after the original data was collected, demonstrated similar figures.[4]

A weary missionary couple, Rolland and Heidi Baker, arrived almost ready to quit their African work. Both were jolted into new motivation; Heidi had to be helped up from the floor seven nights in a row. She said she heard God say in a vision, "Heidi, no matter what you do, there will always be enough." They returned to Mozambique to launch more than ten thousand churches, three primary schools and five Bible schools.

A West Coast pastor, Bill Johnson, came to Toronto. A year later, he was named senior pastor of Bethel Church in Redding, California, which today is known worldwide for its dynamic ministry of healing as well as its worship songs.

A Church of England curate, Nicky Gumbel, came and took the spiritual infusion back to Holy Trinity Brompton in London, where an eleven-week evangelistic course had recently been inaugurated but was not yet flourishing. The trip turned out to be "the kick-start Alpha needed," wrote one secular journalist.[5] Alpha has now spread to nearly every nation of the world, with its materials in 112 languages being used by millions of attendees.

Other observers were not so positive, however, focusing on the externals, such as worshipers becoming so exuberant they even roared with delight. Cult critic Hank Hanegraaff went on his syndicated radio program, *Bible Answer Man*, to decry the goings-on. Popular author John MacArthur hosted a "Strange Fire" conference years later in his California church that made his objections clear.

The Vineyard association was supportive at first, giving counsel to the Arnotts and citing historical precedents from past revivals (the Wesleyan revival across the British Isles, the First and Second Great Awakenings in America, etc.). As the months rolled on and controversies mounted, however, John Wimber became concerned. A Vineyard board report stated in part, "Questionable manifestations have not been the major part of the renewal, but have attracted a disproportionate amount of attention. . . . We would like people to be known as 'evangelists' or 'zealous Christian workers' rather than 'roarers' or 'shakers'."[6] At the end of 1994, the board withdrew its affiliation with Toronto.

John and Carol did not protest; instead, they got busy leading the church to rename itself the "Toronto Airport Christian Fellowship" and continue its ministry for years to come. It should be noted that two decades later (after another name change to "Catch the Fire"), the rift was mended when the Arnotts welcomed Vineyard leader Blaine Cook to the stage of a reunion celebration. Both sides apologized for past hurts and emphasized their respect and love for each other's work.

The passing of time has likewise adjusted the views of Professor James A. Beverley at nearby Tyndale University (formerly Ontario Bible College, where John Arnott studied). In the early days, he had called the renewal a "mixed blessing," but confessed in 2014, "My concerns have changed a bit. I regret saying that they did not give enough attention to Jesus. I think that was too hard. The leaders and the people, they love Jesus. We all do not give enough attention to Jesus."[7]

His fellow academic, John Stackhouse of the University of Manitoba, gives perhaps the most insightful view:

Any outsider trying to estimate spiritual fruit of revivals always has trouble, even with 100 years of history, let alone at the moment. . . . Anglo-Canadians are not renowned for a demonstrative personality. For a middle-aged Anglo-Canadian to quiver, shake, and fall to the ground is pretty incredible. [Christians] now feel social permission to jump into the deep end of the pool. . . .

There is widespread discontent in North American Christianity. Many of us are being asked by churches to settle for "life-support Christianity" instead of thriving Christianity. We should be saying, "Are we missing out on something?"[8]

45

Jim Cymbala
(1943–)

Fresh Wind, Fresh Fire

Kids on the Brooklyn playgrounds learned early that young Jim knew what to do with a basketball in his hands. He was not that tall, but he had an instinct for when to pass, when to stutter-step and when to take the shot himself. At the end of high school, he landed an appointment to the US Naval Academy, where he broke the plebe (freshman) scoring record. Late that first year, a back injury forced him to withdraw from the navy, but the University of Rhode Island quickly gave him an athletic scholarship. The scrappy point guard became team captain his senior year and led the Rams to a March Madness berth.

Back in New York City, he married his former pastor's daughter named Carol, and settled down to a job in the business world of Manhattan. His father-in-law, however, kept giving him books on spiritual topics. The man, now an evangelist as well as overseer of a half-dozen fledgling churches in the metro area, saw potential in the young couple and eventually dared to suggest they might enter the ministry. "I'm not qualified," Jim promptly replied (he had been a sociology major).[1]

But the father-in-law would not give up. He coaxed them first to take on a small congregation in Newark, New Jersey, then later a similar struggling group of fewer than thirty on Atlantic Avenue in Brooklyn. Jim's sermons were skimpy, he knew. But at least Carol could play the piano. They struggled along for a year or two, working second jobs to pay their bills, often ready to quit.

Then, on top of all the other woes, Jim came down with a severe bronchitis he could not shake. Carol's parents finally bought him a plane ticket to fly down to their Florida home and try to recuperate in the warm sunshine. One afternoon he went out on a tourist fishing boat—not to fish, but rather to think.

"Lord, I have no idea how to be a successful pastor," I prayed softly out there on the water. "I haven't been trained. All I know is that Carol and I are working in the middle of New York City, with people dying on every side, overdosing from heroin, consumed by materialism, and all the rest. If the gospel is so powerful . . ."

I couldn't finish the sentence. Tears choked me. Fortunately, the others on the boat were too far away to notice as they studied their lines in the blue-green water.

Then quietly but forcefully, in words heard not with my ear but deep within my spirit, I sensed God speaking:

If you and your wife will lead my people to pray and call upon my name, you will never lack for something fresh to preach. I will supply all the money that's needed, both for the church and for your family, and you will never have a building large enough to contain the crowds I will send in response.[2]

Jim Cymbala returned to Brooklyn, his hacking cough now subsiding, and stood up the very next Sunday to say he had heard from God. As a result, he declared, "From this day on, the prayer meeting will be the barometer of our church. What happens on Tuesday night will be the gauge by which we will judge success or failure because that will be the measure by which God blesses us."[3]

And the rest is history. The steady growth and vitality of the Brooklyn Tabernacle began drawing people to the Savior by the dozens, then hundreds, and then thousands—desperate drug addicts but also uptown professionals, whites, blacks, Hispanics from the Caribbean, teenagers, parents and grandparents. Carol started a choir, despite her lack of any formal music training; she taught everyone's parts by ear. And the engine driving every advance of the Kingdom, Jim kept insisting, was the Tuesday night prayer meeting.

By the early 1990s (when this author first visited), you had to show up an hour or more early to get a seat in the converted theater on Flatbush Avenue. If you waited until the starting hour of seven o'clock, you would be crammed into the lobby watching on a video screen. A slotted box in the entryway welcomed written prayer requests for everything from unemployment to illness to wayward offspring to marriages in trouble. When the crowd began to pray, all in concert, the sound swelled like a home run had just been hit at Yankee Stadium. The Sunday choir did not sing; Pastor Cymbala didn't even preach a sermon on Tuesday nights, but maybe gave just a brief exhortation from the Word. The overall intensity of intercession ruled, reflecting the tough conditions of urban life.

One week, a couple of church members brought a teenage girl who, they told the pastor, was on drugs and needed deliverance. About a half hour into the prayer meeting, he called her forward for prayer. She seemed in a daze—until someone quietly said, "Oh Jesus, help us."

> Like a shot, the mention of Jesus' name brought an explosion of rage and screaming. The five-foot-one-inch girl lunged for my throat, throwing back the two friends who had guided her up the aisle. Before I knew what was happening, I had been body-slammed against the front edge of the platform. Diana ripped the collar right off my white shirt as if it were a piece of tissue. A hideous voice from deep inside her began to scream, "You'll never have her! She's ours! Get away from her!" The language then turned obscene.
>
> Some in the congregation stood and began to pray aloud. Others gasped. Some covered their eyes. Meanwhile, several deacons jumped up and tried to pull her off of me. Despite her size, she fought all of us with tremendous strength.
>
> We finally managed to subdue her. Amy [a visiting evangelist] began to pray fervently. I leaned over the girl to address the spirits: "Shut up! In the name of Jesus, come out of her!" I demanded.
>
> Diana's eyes rolled back in her head, and twice she spit directly into my face, no more than a foot away. The church kept earnestly calling out to God for his help. Clearly, we were not battling some imaginary "spirit of anger" or whatever. This was a classic case of demon possession.
>
> Within a few minutes, the girl was set totally free. She stopped cursing; her body relaxed. We relaxed our grip on her, and she gently stood up to raise her hands and begin praising the Lord. Soon she was singing, with the rest of us, "Oh, the blood of Jesus! It washes white as snow," as tears streamed down her cheeks, ruining her makeup.[4]

Cymbala eventually wrote his first book, *Fresh Wind, Fresh Fire*, which sold slowly at first until word of mouth kicked in, pushing it onto the Christian hardcover bestseller list for more than four years and winning the Christian Book of the Year Award in 2000. Out-of-town visitors began to pour into the church by the busload. Most of them learned they had been mispronouncing his name as *sim-BAH-lah*, assuming he must be of African heritage since he's an inner-city pastor. It is actually *SIM-buh-luh* (his father was Ukrainian, his mother Polish).

Despite his oft-repeated apologies for not going to seminary, readers found him to be well-read as he quoted past giants of the faith: Spurgeon, William Law, E. M. Bounds, Charles G. Finney. Invitations to speak at national conferences kept coming from a wide range of evangelicals—Nazarenes, Southern Baptists, the Moody Bible Institute and its radio network.

Meanwhile, Carol's choir was recording albums, doing special events in New York City's famous Radio City Music Hall as well as Carnegie Hall and winning six Grammy Awards. But the singers weren't just performers up in a choir loft; they had been cross-trained to also serve as Sunday altar counselors, stepping down as their pastor finished his message with a public invitation.

In perhaps his strongest book on the work of the Holy Spirit, entitled *Fresh Power*, he spends an entire chapter contrasting "cemeteries" (churches without spiritual life) with "insane asylums" (peculiar charismatic meetings). In his gutsy Brooklyn style, he challenges everyone to make earnest prayer the center of their life with Christ.

Slick organization, barbecues, and theater productions in the church may have their place, but how in the world will they combat the rampant evil around us today? How will they break the stranglehold of materialism in people's lives? The idea that the church is just a teaching center, or a place to escape from the world, is not the right picture. We have a mission from Jesus Himself, and only the outpouring of the Spirit's power will enable us to make a difference.[5]

46

Wonsuk & Julie Ma
(1949–)/(1955–)

The Scholars

I f you are aspiring to do serious mission research at the PhD level, you could hardly aim higher than the UK's Oxford Centre for Mission Studies (OCMS). Its faculty is world-class, its students come from all corners of the globe, it is housed in an elegant 160-year-old stone cathedral, and the massive University of Oxford libraries (thirty million volumes) are within walking distance.

When in 2005 its Council of Trustees set about to choose the next executive director, it, of course, had any number of British or other Western scholars to consider. But the chair at that time, a well-regarded Methodist bishop from Malaysia, nudged the group to look wider, toward the "Global South" (Latin America, Africa, South Asia, East Asia), where the Christian cause was flourishing. And that is how the OCMS reins fell at last into the hands of a Korean—a Korean Pentecostal, no less.

Dr. Wonsuk Ma's credentials were impeccable: a Bible college degree in his home country, a master of divinity degree from Asia Pacific Theological Seminary in the Philippines (where he subsequently taught) and a doctorate in Old Testament studies from an American seminary (where his dissertation was on "The Spirit of God in Isaiah"). Along the way, he had been the founding president of the Asian Pentecostal Society and its journal. His wife, Julie, had earned her own doctorate and become a respected missiologist.

But the couple had not just cloistered themselves inside ivory towers. During their long sojourn in the Philippines (27 years altogether), they had also plunged into hands-on church planting work among mountain tribes. By the time the call came to move to Oxford, they could count more than 150 churches that had been raised up under their ministry. This meant facing dark resistance head-on at times. Wonsuk explains:

> In the tribal setting, people just naturally expect that spiritual powers are at work in the world. They try to be careful to get a good one on their side rather than an evil one.
>
> So if we didn't bring the powerful work of the Holy Spirit into this setting—confronting sickness or demonic oppression, for example—people would understandably start contrasting our Christianity with their own religion. They would conclude, "Why change?"
>
> That's why in our work we often focused on the village priest—getting into a "power encounter," if you will. We knew that if he came over to the Lord, the whole village would follow. After all, he had been everyone's connection to the spirits![1]

No wonder that when Julia Ma's dissertation was later published, it carried the title *When the Spirit Meets the Spirits*. (She and her husband joked privately that, given their denominational ties all the way back to Korea, she could have called it "When the Assemblies of God Meets the Assembly of 'Gods'"!)

They arrived in Oxford in 2006, firmly believing, in Won-suk's words, that "empowerment is really a part of Christian faith—provided that you don't let your highly crafted theology interfere." They re-engineered the Wednesday morning chapel gathering, which had usually been a brief academic lecture, into a full service of worship, prayer and personal testimony as well as preaching, followed by an all-community lunch.

The couple's own deep spirituality took center stage in the crisis of December 2010. Just as a festive OCMS Christmas party was about to start, word came through that Julie Ma had been rushed to the hospital. The diagnosis there turned out to be dreadful: a brain aneurysm in her frontal lobe. A faculty member, Bill Prevette, recalls:

> I left the party with Dr. David Cranston, an OCMS board member and a top kidney surgeon, to go sit with Wonsuk. The neurosurgeon came out, sat down, and patted him on the knee as he explained that most people with this eruption don't even make it as far as a hospital. If they do, he said, they don't ever regain much mental capacity.
>
> Wonsuk calmly replied, "Well, God has spoken to me about that."
>
> The surgeon looked at all of us and said, "Dr. Ma, Julie's probably not going to recover."
>
> "No," Wonsuk answered, "God spoke to me that we will have many more years and anniversaries together."
>
> About this time, Dr. Cranston walked me out into the hallway and asked, "Is he not able to hear what the surgeon is saying?"
>
> "No, David, I think he's hearing it," I replied. "But remember, he's a Korean Pentecostal! He thinks he's heard from God about this. Let's just wait and see. . . ."

Unbelievably, Julie recovered over the next three months. Wonsuk never wavered. To this day, she is actively teaching alongside her husband.[2]

Wonsuk and Julie spent a full decade at OCMS before moving in 2016 to their third continent, North America. He wanted to get back to more teaching and researching, less administration and fund-raising—but in another broadly based, globally focused environment. That led him to a deanship as the Distinguished Professor of Global Christianity at Oral Roberts University (Tulsa, Oklahoma), which promised he could start building a PhD program there (it opened in 2019). Julie, meanwhile, has received an associate professorship as well.

Their worldview continues to enrich their contributions to academic study. To cite just one example, the editors of *The Cambridge Companion to Pentecostalism* asked Wonsuk to write an overview chapter about the Asian scene. Among his insights:

> I wish to challenge the notion that Pentecostalism in Asia is a transplanted version of the Pentecostal religion "made in the USA." Clear historical links are difficult to establish for some cases.[3]

Then after reviewing five examples, from Korea's "prayer mountains" to Filipino Catholic prayer meetings to Chinese house churches, he concluded:

> If world Christianity is going to grow beyond the one-third level of its population for the first time in history, it has much to do with how Asian Christianity fares in the next decades with the largest population in the world. As about 50 percent of Asian Christians are Pentecostals, this form of Christianity then holds the key to this historic possibility. . . . This is a unique

opportunity. . . . That is where the Spirit's empowerment is expected, I challenge, but with a good amount of human sweat.[4]

Bill Prevette is accurate when he says about his friend Wonsuk Ma, "In addition to being a scholar, he's also something of a mystic! He really has a deep prayer life. When he senses that God has spoken to him, that's it—he's locked in from that point forward.

"Meanwhile, he has a unique ability to bring people together, from all over the map and from many Christian traditions."

From his earliest days in the Philippines, Wonsuk Ma never intended to wear the traditional label "missionary," if that meant someone from a faraway place who embodies their own culture and lives well above the "natives." His paradigm is much broader. He sums it up by writing, "The full understanding of mission in the context of global Christianity will remain my lifelong quest."[5]

47

Cindy Jacobs
(1951–)

The General

Some 3,100 years ago, the Israelites suffered under the heavy thumb of a Canaanite king, until finally "they cried to the LORD for help" (Judges 4:3). In response, God activated their prophet-judge Deborah to organize a resistance, first by recruiting a military commander named Barak. So strong was her leadership that he would not proceed without her at his side. The campaign was a huge success. (The chief Canaanite officer was killed by a cunning woman named Jael, who pounded a sharp tent peg into the side of his head while he slept.)

That's the backstory for the Deborah Company, a collection of charismatic female leaders under the larger umbrella of Dallas-based Generals International, whose website says, "We develop resources and events to equip believers in spiritual warfare, intercession, and the prophetic." Founded in 1985 by Texas speaker and author Cindy Jacobs, the combat motif runs strong throughout its conferences, videos, publications and online courses. When *Charisma* magazine put her on its cover in March 1994, the five-page article headline ran "The Lady Is a General."

Other programs include a Reformation Prayer Network, with nearly fifty "state prayer generals" to encourage intercession. A weekly TV program, *God Knows*, was launched in 2003 after Jacobs grew alarmed on a speaking trip to Spain when she turned on the hotel television set and saw how many fortune-tellers were pitching viewers to call in for information about their futures. She sensed the Lord saying, *I can do better than that. I want to show people the true prophetic gift and My heart for them.*[1] Her weekly program now airs on GOD TV, a British channel that is also seen in North America and other continents. Language options include English, Spanish, Arabic, Hebrew, Russian and Romanian.

Never shy or hesitant, Cindy Jacobs traces her call to ministry all the way back to a quiet afternoon at church camp when she was nine. She says God told her then that He had something special for her to do. Later on, a certain Bible verse stood out to her: "Ask of me, and I shall give thee the heathen for thine inheritance, and the uttermost parts of the earth for thy possession" (Psalm 2:8 KJV). These days, with the full support of her husband, Mike, this "General of Intercession" has developed a global reach through live appearances as well as such books as *Possessing the Gates of the Enemy* and *The Power of Persistent Prayer.*

Her frequent prophecies, often broad in nature on everything from Israel to the coronavirus, are cited on various charismatic websites. However, in other cases her words can be very specific.

Samuel Rodriguez (now president of the NHCLC, see chapter 41) will never forget the day she came to speak at a church he was attempting to start in Sacramento, California. Everything was a struggle there in a repurposed car showroom with curtains covering the garage port doors and an air-conditioning system that could not keep up. The rent was so high that the Rodriguezes were having to make do on a half-salary.

Cindy Jacobs, however, was not tentative in the least. She preached her message that Sunday morning and then added a "word" that this congregation would soon be owning multiple properties—and in addition, would have a television network.

The pastor had to stifle a laugh. The little church had no media presence at all, not even a radio program. And here she was talking about not just a television program, but a whole *network*. Surely not.

On the drive home, Pastor Rodriguez looked at his wife and said, "Well, I'm not doubting it, but . . . that was really an audacious prophecy." They both knew that if any of this was going to happen, it would have to be God's doing all the way.[2]

Within eighteen months, New Season Christian Worship Center's finances had grown strong enough to stop renting and buy a church property on five acres just off a freeway. An Assemblies of God property in the Reno, Nevada, area (140 miles east) was given for a satellite campus. And plans were well along for a 24-hour TV network to be called TBN Salsa, airing nationwide in English for second- and third-generation Hispanic Americans. Who would have expected any of this?

Cindy Jacobs, now entering her seventies, is passionate about reproducing this kind of ministry, through the Deborah Company and multiple other endeavors. It shows brightly in her 2019 book, *Women, Rise Up! A Fierce Generation Taking Its Place in the World*. Straight out of the gate, her opening chapter begins:

> There can be no doubt that God has used and is going to use women in extraordinary ways in every generation. Why do I think this? We women love to fight injustice. From the beginning our Creator said that our seed would bruise the head of the serpent. I believe this is true (see Genesis 3:15). While this might be Messianic in its interpretation, it could also be said of our legacy, both spiritually and physically. There are great injustices around the world that need someone to "dance upon injustice" and rise up and fight.
>
> As I both write my story and highlight the importance of women in leadership and society, I believe there are many issues about which we have been quiet—and need to be "silent no more."[3]

And so, the audacious general forges ever forward.

48

Nicky Gumbel
(1955–)

Mr. Alpha

Persuading skeptical audiences was an art that Nicky Gumbel, the son of two English barristers (lawyers), learned early, even before he went to study law himself at Trinity College, Cambridge. He honed his abilities throughout his twenties while facing juries and judges for six years.

Having converted to Christ during his university days, he left his law practice at the age of 28 to study theology at Oxford. Three years later, he was ordained an Anglican deacon and joined the staff of London's renewal-minded Holy Trinity Brompton church as a curate. The church had a set of classes called Alpha to teach new members the basics of the faith; Gumbel was given responsibility for this in 1990 and proceeded to re-engineer it for the unchurched (or "de-churched," as he called them), of which Britain had plenty. Instead of laying out

Christian propositions—the doctrine of God, of Jesus Christ, of salvation, etc.—he framed the ten sessions around outsiders' questions. The titles:

1. *Is There More to Life Than This?*
2. *Who Is Jesus?*
3. *Why Did Jesus Die?*
4. *How Can I Have Faith?*
5. *Why and How Do I Pray?*
6. *Why and How Should I Read the Bible?*
7. *How Does God Guide Us?*
8. *How Can I Resist Evil?*
9. *Does God Heal Today?*
10. *What about the Church?*[1]

Each week's gathering had three elements: (a) a free meal, (b) a 22- to 28-minute "talk" and (c) freewheeling table discussion about what had been said, with open acceptance of skeptical opinions. (Gumbel's talks have been reproduced in a book, *Questions of Life*, that has now been reprinted dozens of times.)

As Gumbel explained to an interviewer from the *Guardian* newspaper:

> It's a low-key, relaxed, unthreatening, non-confrontational way for people to explore pretty big questions. . . . It's hard to find a place where you can discuss those issues. You can't go down to the pub and say, "What do you think the meaning of life is?" . . . But actually, most people have those questions, somewhere in the back of their minds. And if you can find a place where you can discuss it with a group of people who, like you, are outside

of the Church, and it's a non-threatening, relaxed environment, quite a lot of people want to do that.[2]

One additional element was added along the way: the Alpha "Day Away" for late in the series, when the group would spend a full Saturday, usually at a retreat center outside the city, focusing on "Who Is the Holy Spirit?" In his introductory talk (now on video), Gumbel starts all the way back at Genesis 1, where the Spirit of God "was 'hovering over the waters' . . . just as the Holy Spirit is here today, wanting to bring new things to our lives. When the Spirit comes, he always brings newness, new attitudes, new ways of worship.

"We are conservative by nature, quite cautious about change—especially in the church. But the Holy Spirit is the Creator Spirit."[3]

By the afternoon, Gumbel is inviting people to open up to the Spirit's invasion. He points out that the Greek word *baptizo*, used by John the Baptist to foretell what would happen on the Day of Pentecost, was sometimes applied to a sunken ship in the ocean. "That's what the Spirit wants. He wants to drench us, overwhelm us, fill us."[4] Soon the room begins to swell with the sounds of people speaking in tongues for the first time.

The Alpha course was doing well enough in the early 1990s, but it took a sudden curve upward after Gumbel paid a visit to the Toronto Airport Vineyard in 1994 (see chapter 44). The participant count shot up from 4,500 the previous year to 30,000 . . . then to 100,000 in 1995 . . . a quarter million in 1996 . . . a half million in 1997 . . . a full million two years later. The numbers today are hard to calculate, as Alpha has spread to virtually all denominations (Protestant, Catholic, Orthodox) across 169 countries; its print and video materials have been translated into at least one hundred languages. A parallel set of videos for youth viewers has been released.

Gumbel tries not to get pegged as a "charismatic" or a "Pentecostal" or even an "evangelical," for that matter. He simply wants to be known as a "Christian." If a reporter pushes him to state *what kind* of Christian he is, the only answer he will give is "Anglican." That is because his vision is global and trans-sectarian; he wants to draw people from all traditions and cultures into a living walk with Christ.

When the *Guardian* interviewer (a self-confessed atheist) drilled down on the tongues component, Gumbel calmly answered:

> I think it's a form of prayer which comes from the Holy Spirit, and it's there in the Book of Acts and there in the history of the Church. I can give you a book by the preacher to the Pope [Fr. Raniero Cantalamessa, a Franciscan friar], where he talks about this experience. It's something that he's experienced himself, and it's common throughout the different parts of the Church. It's not a huge emphasis in the New Testament, and I don't think it's a huge emphasis [in] Alpha. I hope it's not . . . because it shouldn't be.[5]

The video on healing (ninth in the series) includes not only instruction on praying for the sick, but also stunning examples: a young woman stricken with fungal meningitis and given just eight weeks to live being restored overnight after her pastor prayed for her . . . a Down syndrome baby with a hole in his heart and doctors wanting to unplug life support who is now a healthy 27-year-old . . . a basketball player with severe knee damage who, after receiving prayer in an Alpha meeting, went out the next day for a six-mile run.

When Holy Trinity Brompton's vicar, Sandy Millar, retired in 2005, the bishop elevated Gumbel to succeed him. The church today draws more than four thousand per Sunday. It runs its own Alpha courses three times a year, with three hundred to four hundred participating each round. An agnostic newspaper reporter wrote back in 2000, "At a cautious estimate, in Britain alone and in less than a decade, a quarter of a million agnostics have found God through Gumbel."[6] The tally would be much higher today, in part because, as he sometimes says when he does his opening talk live . . .

> Now some of you may be thinking, "Help! What have I got my-self into?" Don't worry. We're not going to pressurize you into doing anything. Perhaps some of you are sitting there sneering. If you are, please don't think that I'm looking down at you. I spent half my life as an atheist. I used to go to talks like this and I would sneer.[7]

The winsome, smiling ex-barrister goes on from there, impervious to misgivings, secure in the knowledge that God has commissioned him to make a strong case for empowered faith. And so far, the juries keep voting yes.

49

Mike Bickle

(1955–)

Twenty-Four/Seven

The *Guinness World Records* book does not have a category called "Longest Nonstop Prayer Meeting." But if it did, there is little doubt the title would go to Kansas City's International House of Prayer (IHOP), where prayer with live worship music has been underway around the clock since the morning of September 19, 1999.

Yes, you read that right. In fact, you can even watch online (www.ihopkc.org/prayerroom) as teams of ten or so singers and instrumentalists lead free-flowing worship in two-hour shifts, from morning to evening and on through the night until the sun comes up again. Worshipers come and go to sit (or stand, or kneel) in the atmosphere of drawing closer to God. Nothing is preprogrammed; there is no "order of service." The goal is simply to enter into the divine Presence as deeply as possible.

Occasionally a staff intercessor may come to the microphone and focus everyone's attention by saying, "Such-and-such a mission organization is doing a special outreach this week in Germany (or Fiji, or Rwanda). Let's obey what Jesus said about praying for spiritual fruit in this harvest field of the world. . . ." Fervent prayer then follows, as the musical underlay continues for an extended time.

Whose idea was this, anyway? Mike Bickle, IHOP's founder-director, admits:

> In my younger days I loved Jesus, but I dreaded spending time in prayer. I saw prayer as a necessary duty that I had to endure if I wanted to receive more blessing. . . .
>
> In the summer of 1974 one of my youth leaders exhorted me to set aside an hour every day for prayer, and I determined to try. I was a freshman at the University of Missouri, living in a student apartment with three other believers. I told them, "I will pray an hour a day, even if it kills me." My announcement brought an element of accountability, knowing that each night they would watch me to see if I actually kept my commitment. So I set my prayer time from nine to ten each night. I referred to it as the "hour of death" because it was so boring. I felt as if I was going to die.[1]

Over time, however, Bickle grew in understanding the value of prayer and how it could enrich his relationship with God. He became a pastor, first in St. Louis and then in Kansas City. The church he founded in 1982 (Kansas City Fellowship) got off to a healthy start. Then the next year, a rather strange-looking prophet stopped by to quote Psalm 27:4: "'One thing have I desired of the LORD, that will I seek after; that I may dwell in the house of the LORD all the days of my life, to behold the beauty of the LORD, and to enquire in his temple'" (KJV). He then followed up by saying, "I'm going to tell you where you're going in the future. You're going to have 24-hour prayer with singers and musicians . . ." He then went on to tell four other predictions.

Bickle could not imagine any of them. When Jones asked him if he was musical, the young pastor shook his head no. The prophet then said, "The Lord told me you'd be dull. I didn't think you'd be *this* dull!"[2]

But Bickle began to study the idea of extended prayer in Scripture as well as throughout church history. He noticed that King David organized and paid 4,000 musicians and 288 singers to lead worship in the temple at least twice a day (2 Chronicles 23–25). Psalm 134 instructed, "Praise the LORD, all you servants of the LORD who minister by night in the house of the LORD. Lift up your hands in the sanctuary and praise the LORD" (verses 1–2).

Then in the New Testament, he came to the elderly Anna, who "never left the temple but worshiped night and day, fasting and praying" (Luke 2:37). The book of Revelation told about four living creatures and 24 elders who "fell down before the Lamb. Each one had a harp and they were holding golden bowls full of incense, which are the prayers of God's people" (Revelation 5:8).

Mike Bickle began to speak about a "harp and bowl" metaphor for serious worship: music combined with an ever-rising aroma of prayer. But not until 1999 did he take the bold step of resigning his pastorate and launching IHOP. Young people began coming from far and wide to serve as "intercessory missionaries," raising their own funds to live on the complex east of downtown Kansas City. Christian leaders such as Bill Bright (Campus Crusade for Christ) and Loren Cunningham

(YWAM) gave their endorsements, appreciating IHOP's prayer support for their ministries.

Meanwhile, the singers and instrumentalists began to see how their giftings could be useful for more than just a four-minute song on Sunday morning or an occasional concert. They found themselves immersed in ministry seven days (and nights) of the week.

As time has passed, Christians in other places have inquired about starting similar houses of prayer in their cities. Bickle encourages this so long as it is organic and local; he has no desire to "franchise" IHOP. The Kansas City model, however, has spread across the United States and well into other nations around the globe.

For a few years, IHOP-KC sponsored a four-day conference in Kansas City's Bartle Hall Convention Center. It would not even advertise headline speakers or worship leaders ahead of time, yet it drew as many as 25,000 attenders, mostly young adults. But after the 2018 event, Bickle called for a "pause," feeling that the work of producing such a huge event had started to overshadow the core calling. "We need time to forge a deeper connection with the Lord, with a renewed zeal and love for Jesus *and* one another in the robust, raw, real context of family," he wrote on IHOP's website. "We want to grow in a deeper vibrancy in our spirit, to receive and share deep insights on the beauty of Jesus, and to sing new songs with a renewed love."[3]

Whatever the format, Mike Bickle is a man zeroed in on the preeminent value of intimacy with God. "The Lord wants much more from His people than for them to be His workforce," he writes. "He longs to have relationship with those who love Him and to partner with them in accomplishing His purposes."[4]

50

Robert Morris

(1961–)

The Explainer

Whenever the Holy Spirit does something out of the ordinary, questions and opinions sprout up. That is certainly what happened on the Day of Pentecost. The crowd outside the upper room was "amazed and perplexed," asking each other, "What does this mean?" Others "made fun of them and said, 'They have had too much wine.'"

Thank God there was a newly Spirit-filled man who stood up at that moment and said, "Let me explain this to you; listen carefully to what I say" (Acts 2:12–14).

One of the clearest explainers of the Spirit's activity in our time is Robert Morris, founding pastor of Gateway Church in the Dallas/Fort Worth metroplex. Perhaps that is partly due to the fact that he didn't grow up in a Pentecostal or charismatic climate. In fact, as a newly saved teenager about to head off to Bible college, his evangelical pastor warned him, "Watch out for people who talk about the Holy Spirit."[1] He followed that advice throughout his education and well into a decade or more of pastoral ministry.

His and his wife's eventual engagement with the baptism and gifts of the Spirit is told in his 2011 book, *The God I Never Knew—How Real Friendship with the Holy Spirit Can Change Your Life*. Step by step, logical piece by logical piece, he unpacks who the Spirit is and how He wants to empower every Christian, if welcomed to do so.

> In the first few years after founding the church I pastor, people frequently asked me, "So, what kind of church is it? Is it Charismatic?" I always prefaced my answer with, "Well, that depends on what you mean by Charismatic."
>
> I'd continue, "If you want to know if we believe in the present person and work of the Holy Spirit, then the answer is definitely yes. If you want to know if we believe that all the gifts of the Holy Spirit mentioned in the New Testament are still available and operating today, again the answer is yes. But some things that you might have seen on television or in other churches that have become associated with the word *charismatic,* I'm not comfortable with. That's definitely *not* who we are as a church."[2]

Authentic life in the Spirit is not just theory for Morris; he openly practices what he preaches, inviting people to open up to the Spirit's immersion and begin to experience spiritual gifts for themselves. His personal stories show this happening in vivid color:

> One Sunday I had just concluded my message and invited those who wanted to receive Christ or needed prayer to come forward to the altar. A number of people were responding to that

call, but my eyes fell upon one gentleman in particular. To my knowledge, I had never seen him before, and there was nothing about his facial expression or manner that would indicate why he was coming forward.

Nevertheless, as I looked at him, I heard the familiar voice of the Holy Spirit telling me something. I knew from experience that the Spirit reveals such things only because He wants to heal, restore, encourage, and bless. So I stepped toward the man and said, "Sir, as you were coming forward, the Lord told me something He wants you to know. He told me that you feel like the prodigal son, because you have been away from Him for a very long time. He just wanted me to give you a message from Him—'Welcome home, son.'"

Instantly the man's eyes filled with tears, and he fell into my arms. On behalf of the father who ran out to meet the returning prodigal of Jesus's parable, I put him in a bear hug that depicted in tangible terms the loving, forgiving embrace that awaits every person who turns to God.[3]

It turned out that the man, who had not been to a church for nearly twenty years, had said to his wife in the parking lot before going inside, "I'm like the prodigal son. But I just don't know if God will really have me back. I'm afraid."

This kind of compassionate, honest, Spirit-led ministry has something to do with why Gateway is now ranked by *Outreach* magazine as the third largest church in America, with more than 31,000 participants spread over nine campuses.[4] It also has congregations in two large Texas prisons. In 2013–2014, Jack Hayford (see chapter 36) agreed to move his fully accredited King's University with its sixteen degree programs (both undergraduate and graduate level) from Southern California to Gateway, naming Morris as its chancellor. The Hayford papers have now been archived there as well.

Meanwhile, Gateway's worship music is widely copied, having risen to uppermost spots on *Billboard*'s Top Christian Albums chart. Morris's messages are repackaged into half-hour TV programs that air in 190 countries. His book *The Blessed Life: Unlocking the Rewards of Generous Living* has become a perennial bestseller.

Yet, with all this attention, Robert Morris shows no signs of turning generic. His church's website continues to carry a lengthy (1,350 words) position paper on "The Baptism in the Holy Spirit." Among its levelheaded statements are these:

> We recognize that the families and members of Gateway Church come from varied and diverse backgrounds. As such, we extend the opportunity for people to grow in their understanding of the person and power of the Holy Spirit. . . . No one will ever be forced to receive the Holy Spirit or any of His gifts, but all are taught the contemporary work of the Holy Spirit from Scripture. . . .
>
> Jesus promised His Church that they would receive a powerful encounter with the Holy Spirit after Jesus' own death and resurrection. It is our view that God desires every Christian to experience this same encounter with the Holy Spirit's power. . . .
>
> While we acknowledge that emotionalism has often been associated with expressions of the Holy Spirit and at times there has been failure in the church universal to properly administrate the manifestations of the Holy Spirit, we do not think these are sufficient reasons to limit the work or expression of the Holy Spirit at Gateway Church. . . . [5]

Ever the careful explainer, Robert Morris continues to lead skeptics and enthusiasts alike into a genuine, growing friendship with the Spirit of God.

Notes

Chapter 2 Smith Wigglesworth

1. Various accounts of this prophecy were published over the years. One of the most extensive is found at www. http://www.smithwigglesworth.com /pensketches/prophecy.html.

Chapter 3 Charles H. Mason

1. https://en.wikipedia.org/wiki/Charles_Harrison_Mason, citing *Church of God in Christ Official Manual 1973*, Memphis, Tenn.
2. Ibid.

Chapter 4 William J. Seymour

1. Frank Bartleman, *What Really Happened at Azusa Street* (Northridge, Calif.: Voice Christian Publications, 1962), 33.
2. Harvey Cox, *Fire from Heaven* (Reading, Mass.: Addison-Wesley, 1995), 262.

Chapter 5 John G. Lake

1. Gordon Lindsay, comp., *John G. Lake—Apostle to Africa* (Dallas: Christ For The Nations, 1972), 25.
2. Ibid.
3. http://www.scielo.org.za/scielo.php?script=sci_arttext&pid=S1017-04 992016000100006.
4. Lindsay, *John G. Lake,* 9.

Chapter 6 F. F. Bosworth

1. F. F. Bosworth, *Christ the Healer* (Grand Rapids, Mich.: Chosen, 2008 edition), 22.
2. Ibid., 69.

Chapter 7 Francisco Olazábal

1. www.peopleinchargeofchange.com/this-day-in-history-francisco-olazabal.

Chapter 8 Aimee Semple McPherson

1. Cited in Cox, *Fire from Heaven*, 126–27.
2. Aimee Semple McPherson, *This Is That* (Los Angeles: International Church of the Foursquare Gospel, 1923) as reprinted by *Charisma* magazine, April 2006, 81.
3. Ibid., 82.

Chapter 9 J. E. Stiles

1. Albert Hibbert, *Smith Wigglesworth: The Secret of His Power* (Tulsa, Okla.: Harrison House, 1982), 68.
2. J. E. Stiles, *The Gift of the Holy Spirit* (Myersville, Md.: Art Williams, 1985 reprint), 104.

Chapter 10 Donald Gee

1. Donald Gee, "Pentecost Is for All," *Pentecostal Evangel,* May 4, 1969, 7.
2. "Extremes Are Sometimes Necessary," https://www.tonycooke.org/riches-from-history/extremes-are-sometimes-necessary/, reprinted from a 1953 article in *The Voice of Healing.*

Chapter 11 Agnes Sanford

1. Agnes Sanford, *Sealed Orders* (Alachua, Fla.: Bridge-Logos, 1972), 97.
2. Ibid., 102–3.
3. Agnes Sanford, *The Healing Light* (Plainfield, N.J.: Logos edition, 1972), 15–16.
4. http://heyjoi.tripod.com,
5. Sanford, *Healing Light,* 29–31.

Chapter 12 Leo Josef Suenens

1. "The Pentecostal Tide," *Time*, June 18, 1973, 93.

2. Michael Harper, *Let My People Grow* (Plainfield, N.J.: Logos, 1975), 96, citing Gabriel Murphy F.S.C., *Charisma and Church Renewal* (n.p.: Officium Libri Catholici, 1965), 105–07.

3. Leo Josef Suenens, *A New Pentecost?* (London: Darton, Longmen and Todd, 1975), 212.

4. *Time,* "The Pentecostal Tide," 93.

5. Peter Steinfels, "Leo Joseph Cardinal Suenens, A Vatican II Leader, Dies at 91," *New York Times*, May 7, 1996, https://www.nytimes.com/1996/05/07/world/leo-joseph-cardinal-suenens-a-vatican-ii-leader-dies-at-91.html.

6. *Time,* "The Pentecostal Tide," 93.

Chapter 13 David du Plessis

1. David du Plessis, *The Spirit Bade Me Go* (Alachua, Fla.: Bridge-Logos, 2004 edition), 10.

2. Cecil M. Robeck Jr. "The Charismatic Renewal of the Church," *Theology, News and Notes,* March 1983, 3.

3. Robeck, "Charismatic Renewal," 4–5.

Chapter 14 Gordon and Freda Lindsay

1. www.williambranhamhomepage.org/masent14.htm.

2. *The Voice of Healing,* April 1948, 1.

3. www.cfni.org.

Chapter 15 Kathryn Kuhlman

1. *Time,* "Miracle Woman," September 14, 1970, 62.

2. Jamie Buckingham, *Daughter of Destiny* (Plainfield, N.J.: Logos, 1976), 55–56.

3. Grant Wacker, "The Forgotten Female Preacher," *Christianity Today,* October 2018, 47.

4. As quoted by Wacker in "The Forgotten Female Preacher," 48.

Chapter 16 Leonard Ravenhill

1. Leonard Ravenhill, *Why Revival Tarries* (Minneapolis: Bethany, 1959), 1.

2. Ibid., 4.

3. Ibid., x–xi.

4. Endorsement for *In Light of Eternity: The Life of Leonard Ravenhill* by Mack Tomlinson (Hannibal, Mo.: Granted Ministries Press, 2019).

5. Ibid.

6. Ravenhill, *Why Revival Tarries*, 34.

Chapter 17 William Branham

1. William Branham, "How the Gift Came to Me," *The Voice of Healing*, April 1948, 8.

2. https://william-branham.org/site/people/ern_baxter.

3. "William Marrion Branham," *The New International Dictionary of Pentecostal and Charismatic Movements,* rev. and expanded ed. (Grand Rapids, Mich.: Zondervan, 2003), citing W. J. Hollenweger, *The Pentecostals* (Minneapolis: Augsburg, 1972).

Chapter 19 Derek Prince

1. https://www.charismamag.com/site-archives/154-peopleevents/people-and-events/1069.

2. Jamie Buckingham, "The End of the Discipleship Era," *Ministries Today,* January/February 1980, 50.

3. Ibid.

Chapter 20 Dennis and Rita Bennett

1. Dennis Bennett, *Nine O'Clock in the Morning,* as cited in Vinson Synan, *The Century of the Holy Spirit* (Nashville: Thomas Nelson, 2001), 152.

2. Vinson Synan, *The Century of the Holy Spirit* (Nashville: Thomas Nelson, 2001), 153.

3. As reprinted in "Why the Baptism in the Holy Spirit?" *Charisma*, April 2006, 86.

4. Ibid., 88.

5. Dennis J. Bennett, "They Spoke with Tongues and Magnified God!" *The Mantle,* July 1963, 5.

6. See www.emotionallyfree.org.

Chapter 21 Kenneth E. Hagin

1. Gordon D. Fee, "The Disease of the Health & Wealth Gospels," *Agora* magazine, republished by The Word for Today, Costa Mesa, Calif., 1979, 11.

2. Kenneth E. Hagin, *The Midas Touch* (Tulsa, Okla.: Faith Library Publications, 2000).

Chapter 22 Harald Bredesen

1. John L. Sherrill, *They Speak with Other Tongues* (New York: McGraw-Hill, 1964), 12.

2. Ibid., 13–14.

Chapter 23 Oral Roberts

1. Oral Roberts, *My Story* (self-published, 1961), 3.
2. Ibid., 35.
3. Jack Gould, "On Faith Healing," *New York Times,* February 19, 1956.
4. Randy Frame, "Did Oral Roberts Go Too Far?" *Christianity Today,* February 20, 1987.

Chapter 24 Tommy Tyson

1. *The Works of John Wesley,* third edition complete and unabridged (Grand Rapids, Mich.: Baker, 1998), 1:170 (entry for January 1, 1739).
2. Tom Ivy, "Remembering Tommy Tyson," Testimonials, Tommy Tyson, accessed September 29, 2020, https://tommytyson.org/testimonials/.

Chapter 25 T. L. and Daisy Osborn

1. T. L. Osborn, *3 Keys to the Book of Acts* (self-published, 1960), 15–16.
2. Ibid., 53–54.

Chapter 26 John and Elizabeth Sherrill

1. Sherrill, *Other Tongues,* 11–12.
2. Ibid., 27.
3. Ibid., 29.
4. Ibid., 140–141.

Chapter 27 Francis and Judith MacNutt

1. Francis MacNutt, *Healing* (Notre Dame, Ind.: Ave Maria Press, 1974), 17–18.
2. MacNutt, *The Power to Heal* (Notre Dame, Ind.: Ave Maria Press, 1977), 29.
3. Ibid., 39.
4. Julia Duin, "Catholics on the Pentecostal Trail," *Christianity Today,* June 22, 1992, 26.

Chapter 28 Bernard E. Underwood and Ithiel Clemmons

1. J. Lee Grady, "Pentecostals Renounce Racism," *Christianity Today,* December 12, 1994, 58.
2. "The Memphis Manifesto," excerpted in *Ministries Today* (January/February 1995), 38.
3. Reprinted in Dean Merrill, *Miracle Invasion* (Savage, Minn.: Broad-Street, 2018), 182–83.

4. See Ithiel Clemmons, "The Urgency of Our Task," *Ministries Today* (January/February 1995), 44.

Chapter 29 Larry Christenson

1. As quoted in Synan, *Century*, 161.
2. As reported in "Lutheran Charismatics," *New International Dictionary*, 847.
3. Duin, "Catholics on the Charismatic Trail," 26.
4. *Trinity* magazine, vol. III, no. 1, as cited in Sherrill, *Other Tongues*, 86.

Chapter 30 Pat Robertson

1. David Edwin Harrell Jr., *Pat Robertson: A Life and Legacy* (Grand Rapids, Mich.: Eerdmans, 2010).
2. Ibid., 273.

Chapter 31 Everett L. "Terry" Fullam

1. Bob Slosser, *Miracle in Darien* (Plainfield, N.J.: Logos, 1979), 58.
2. Slosser, *Miracle*, 78.
3. As quoted in David W. Virtue, "An Interview with Terry Fullam," VirtueOnline, January 19, 2004, www.virtueonline.org/interview-terry-fullam.
4. For the full story of Fullam's own baptism in the Spirit eleven years earlier under the ministry of Fr. Dennis Bennett, see Slosser, *Miracle,* 46–53.
5. Slosser, *Miracle,* 75–76.
6. Ibid., 87.
7. "The View from Above," *Leadership Journal*, Winter 1984, 13.
8. "View," *Leadership Journal*, 22.

Chapter 32 C. Peter Wagner

1. C. Peter Wagner, "MC 510: Signs, Wonders and Church Growth," *Christian Life,* October 1982, 44.
2. C. Peter Wagner, *What Are We Missing?* (Carol Stream, Ill.: Creation House, 1978).
3. "MC 510," *Christian Life,* 46.
4. Ibid.
5. C. Peter Wagner, *Our Kind of People: The Ethical Dimension of Church Growth in America* (Richmond, Va.: John Knox, 1978).
6. These were originally published by Regal Books. They now appear under the Chosen Books brand.
7. David Allan Hubbard, "Hazarding the Risks," *Christian Life,* October 1982, 36.

8. For one example, see Jim Cymbala's chapter on "The Lure of Novelty" in *Fresh Wind, Fresh Fire* (Grand Rapids, Mich.: Zondervan, 1997), specifically pp. 106–107 and 114.

9. C. Peter Wagner, *Apostles Today* (Ventura, Calif.: Regal, 2006).

10. C. Peter Wagner, *Dominion!* (Minneapolis: Chosen, 2008), back cover.

11. https://www.christianitytoday.com/edstetzer/2016/october/in-memory-of-c-peter-wagner.html.

Chapter 33 Michael Harper

1. Michael Harper, *None Can Guess* (London: Hodder and Stoughton, 1971), 13.

2. Ibid., 15.

3. Ibid., 21.

4. Ibid., 47.

5. Ibid., 50.

6. Ibid., 54–55.

7. Ibid., 60–61, 63.

8. Michael Harper, "Pentecost or Babel?" a *Renewal* article reprinted in the June 1985 issue of *New Covenant*, 7.

9. Michael Harper, *Let My People Grow* (Plainfield, N.J.: Logos, 1977), 113.

Chapter 34 David Wilkerson

1. David Wilkerson with John and Elizabeth Sherrill, *The Cross and the Switchblade* (Minneapolis: Chosen, 2008), 80.

2. Ibid., 200.

3. Goof balls are capsules that combine barbiturates with amphetamines.

4. Wilkerson, *Switchblade*, 200–201.

5. Ibid., 214–15.

6. Robert Crosby, "Remembering David Wilkerson," www.christianitytoday.com/ct/2011/aprilweb-only/rememberingdavidwilkerson.html.

7. Nicky Cruz, "David Wilkerson 'Never Lost His Heart,'" interview by Trevor Persaud, *Christianity Today*, April 29, 2011, https://www.christianitytoday.com/ct/2011/aprilweb-only/nickycruz.html.

Chapter 35 Jamie Buckingham

1. Jamie Buckingham, *Where Eagles Soar* (Lincoln, Va.: Chosen, 1980), 31.

2. Ibid., 33.

3. Buckingham, "Let the Bread Bake Awhile," *National Courier*, September 2, 1977.

4. Buckingham, *Eagles*, 33.

Chapter 36 Jack Hayford

1. Jack Hayford, *The Church on the Way* (Lincoln, Va.: Chosen, 1982), 18.
2. Ibid., 31.
3. Jack Hayford, *The Beauty of Spiritual Language* (Dallas: Word, 1992), 14.
4. Ibid., 153.
5. All three quotations come from Tim Stafford, "The Pentecostal Gold Standard," *Christianity Today*, July 2005, 24–29.

Chapter 37 Bill Hamon

1. See 1 Corinthians 11:4–5; 12:10; also Paul's encouragement to the whole Corinthian congregation to prophesy (14:1, 5, 31, 39).
2. Bill Hamon, *Your Highest Calling* (Minneapolis: Chosen, 2019), 132.
3. Bill Hamon, *Prophets and Personal Prophecy* (Shippensburg, Pa.: Destiny Image, 1987), 73. This book is perhaps his fullest exposition of personal prophecy.
4. Ibid., 84.
5. Ibid., 151.
6. See www.christianinternational.com.
7. Hamon, *Personal Prophecy*, 106.
8. Wayne Grudem, *The Gift of Prophecy in the New Testament and Today*, rev. ed. (Wheaton, Ill.: Crossway, 2000), 323–324.

Chapter 38 John Wimber

1. John Wimber with Kevin Springer, *Power Healing* (San Francisco: Harper & Row, 1987), 51–52.
2. Forum on "The Church: Healing's Natural Home?" *Leadership Journal*, Spring 1985, 122.
3. See Bill Jackson's *The Quest for the Radical Middle: A History of the Vineyard* (Anaheim, Calif.: Vineyard International Publishing, 1999).
4. Wimber, *Power Healing*, 237.
5. "Wonder-working Power," *Christianity Today*, March 19, 1990, 29–30.
6. Today the Association of Vineyard Churches numbers more than 2,400 congregations in ninety countries.
7. "Refreshing, Renewal, and Revival," *Vineyard Reflections* newsletter, July/August 1994, 1.
8. Ibid., 2.

Chapter 39 Jane Hansen Hoyt

1. Jane Hansen, *The Journey of a Woman* (Ventura, Calif.: Regal, 1998), 40, 42.
2. Ibid., 70.

3. Ibid., 71.
4. Ibid., 140.

Chapter 40 David Mainse

1. Mainse was a graduate of Eastern Pentecostal Bible College and was ordained by the Pentecostal Assemblies of Canada (PAOC).
2. As told on "Remembering David Mainse" (see www.youtube.com/wa tch?v=b5jX4RM6hFl).
3. Debra Fieguth and Lloyd Mackey, "A Promise for the Nations," *Christian Herald*, September 1986, 18.
4. Ron Csillag, "Canadian televangelist David Mainse was the friendly face of 100 Huntley Street," *Globe and Mail*, October 4, 2017, https://www .theglobeandmail.com/arts/television/canadian-televangelist-david-mainse -was-the-friendly-face-of-100-huntley-street/article36494463/.
5. Karl Vaters, *Pivot* blog, https://christianitytoday.com/karl-vaters/2017/ september/conversation-with-david-mainse.html/.

Chapter 41 Jesse Miranda

1. Jeff M. Sellers, "You Can Take the Boy Out of the Barrio . . .," *Christianity Today*, September 9, 2002.
2. Ibid.
3. Ibid.
4. Morgan Lee, "Died: Jesse Miranda, Hispanic Evangelicals' Bridge-Builder," *Christianity Today,* July 18, 2019, https://www.christianitytoday .com/news/2019/july/died-jesse-miranda-hispanic-evangelicals-pentecostals -amen.html.
5. Ibid.
6. Jesse Miranda, "Modern Samaritans," *Christianity Today*, May 16, 2013, https://www.christianitytoday.com/ct/2013/may-web-only/modern -samaritans.html.
7. Ibid.

Chapter 42 Reinhard Bonnke

1. *The 700 Club* with Pat Robertson, February 1, 2018.
2. nowlistening, "Raised from the Dead! by Reinhard Bonnke—Part 1 of 6," YouTube video, posted October 7, 2008, https://www.youtube.com/wa tch?v=SroD02bP120.
3. Kate Shellnutt, "Died: Reinhard Bonnke, Record-Setting Evangelist to Africa," News and Reporting, *Christianity Today*, December 7, 2019, https:// www.christianitytoday.com/news/2019/december/reinhard-bonnke-died-eva ngelist-christ-for-all-nations-afri.html.

Chapter 43 Kevin and Dorothy Ranaghan

1. https://www1.cbn.com/fifty-years-catholic-charismatic-movement-1967–2017.
2. Ibid.
3. Bert Ghezzi, as quoted in Vinson Synan, *In the Latter Days: The Outpouring of the Holy Spirit in the Twentieth Century* (self-pub., Xulon, 2001).
4. Expressed in various writings, including Karen Wullenweber, "Catholic Pentecostals," *St. Anthony Messenger* (January 1969), 21.
5. Ibid., 20.
6. Ibid., 26.

Chapter 44 John and Carol Arnott

1. John Arnott, "The Toronto Blessing: What Is It?" *John and Carol*, December 31, 1999, www.johnandcarol.org/updates/the-toronto-blessing-what-is-it.
2. John Arnott, "John and Carol Arnott: Soaking in the Spirit," interview by Pat Robertson, *The 700 Club*, CBN video, accessed September 29, 2020, https://www1.cbn.com/700club/john-and-carol-arnott-soaking-spirit.
3. Lorna Dueck, "The Enduring Revival," *Christianity Today*, March 7, 2014, https://www.christianitytoday.com/ct/2014/march-web-only/enduring-revival.html.
4. As reported in her "Toronto Blessing" entry in *New International Dictionary*, 1150, which drew upon her original *The Toronto Report* (1996) and "The 'Toronto Blessing': Charisma, Institutionalization and Revival," published in the *Journal for the Scientific Study of Religion* 36 (June 2, 1997).
5. Jon Ronson, "Catch Me If You Can," *Guardian*, October 20, 2000, https://www.theguardian.com/theguardian/2000/oct/21/weekend7.weekend.
6. "Board Report," Association of Vineyard Churches, September/October 1994, 1–2.
7. As quoted in Lorna Dueck, "The Enduring Revival," *Christianity Today*, March 7, 2014, https://www.christianitytoday.com/ct/2014/march-web-only/enduring-revival.html.
8. "Toronto Blessing: Is It a Revival?" *Christianity Today*, May 15, 1995, https://www.christianitytoday.com/ct/1995/may15/5t6051.html.

Chapter 45 Jim Cymbala

1. Jim Cymbala with Dean Merrill, *Fresh Wind, Fresh Fire* (Grand Rapids, Mich.: Zondervan, 1997), 13.
2. Cymbala, *Fresh Wind*, 25.
3. Ibid., 27.
4. Cymbala, *Fresh Wind*, 109–110.
5. Jim Cymbala with Dean Merrill, *Fresh Power* (Grand Rapids, Mich.: Zondervan, 2001), 38.

Chapter 46 Wonsuk and Julie Ma

1. Wonsuk Ma, personal interview with the author, April 29, 2020.

2. Bill Prevette, personal interview with the author, April 22, 2020.

3. Wonsuk Ma, "Asian Pentecostalism in Context: A Challenging Portrait," *The Cambridge Companion to Pentecostalism*, edited by Cecil M. Robeck Jr. and Amos Yong (New York: Cambridge University Press, 2014), 152.

4. Ibid., 167–168.

5. Wonsuk Ma, "My Pilgrimage in Mission," *International Bulletin of Mission Research*, vol. 40(4) 340–348.

Chapter 47 Cindy Jacobs

1. "About God Knows," Generals International, accessed September 29, 2020, www.generals.org/about-god-knows.

2. Dean Merrill, *Miracle Invasion* (Savage, Minn.: BroadStreet, 2018), 172–173.

3. Cindy Jacobs, *Women, Rise Up!* (Minneapolis: Chosen, 2019), 19.

Chapter 48 Nicky Gumbel

1. "Alpha Film Series," Alpha, accessed September 29, 2020, https://www.alpha.org/preview/alpha-film-series/.

2. "Nicky Gumbel Interview Transcript," interview by Adam Rutherford, August 28, 2009, https://www.theguardian.com/commentisfree/belief/2009/aug/28/religion-christianity-alpha-gumbel-transcript.

3. Nicky Gumbel, "Talk 1—Who Is the Holy Spirit? (1/2)," posted by Rahelle Tseng, YouTube video, March 29, 2012, https://www.youtube.com/watch?v=qsSc2qljZSU.

4. Nicky Gumbel, "Talk 2—Who Is the Holy Spirit? (2/2)," posted by Rahelle Tseng, YouTube video, March 29, 2012, https://www.youtube.com/watch?v=6S3r24S9Xrg.

5. "Nicky Gumbel Interview Transcript."

6. Ronson, "Catch Me If You Can."

7. Ibid.

Chapter 49 Mike Bickle

1. Mike Bickle, *Growing in Prayer: A Real-Life Guide to Talking with God* (Lake Mary, Fla.: Charisma, 2014), 2.

2. To watch this story as Bickle told it 35 years later on *The Jim Bakker Show*, see www.youtube.com/watch?v=rExwuePliDY.

3. Mike Bickle, "Why This Is Our Last Onething Conference for Some Years," IHOPKC, October 26, 2018, https://www.ihopkc.org/resources/blog/last-onething-conference.

4. Bickle, *Growing in Prayer*, 6.

Chapter 50 Robert Morris

1. Robert Morris, *The God I Never Knew* (Colorado Springs: Water-Brook, 2011), 2.

2. Ibid., 117.

3. Ibid., 25.

4. "Gateway Church: Southlake, Texas," Outreach 100, accessed September 29, 2020, https://outreach100.com/churches/gateway-church.

5. "The Baptism in the Holy Spirit," Gateway Church, accessed September 29, 2020, https://gatewaypeople.com/the-baptism-in-the-holy-spirit.

Dean Merrill had the advantage of being born into a godly home where the Bible was not only read but memorized, and where heroes of the faith were lifted up. He made his personal commitment to Christ at a young age and entered into Spirit fullness not long after. Following high school, he enrolled at Chicago Bible College, where he earned a bachelor's degree in theology.

His ministry calling turned out to be writing and editing, first at a youth magazine (*Campus Life*) and subsequently at *Leadership* (a pastors' journal of Christianity Today, Inc.). Next came the editorship of *Christian Herald*, followed by the Focus on the Family magazine group, which he led as vice president. Along the way, he earned a master's degree in religious publishing at Syracuse University's Newhouse School of Journalism.

As a freelance writer, his work has been published in some forty Christian magazines, including a series of columns in the *Pentecostal Evangel* (Assemblies of God). He served on the board of the Evangelical Press Association and was its president for a term in the late 1980s.

He ventured into curriculum development during a seven-year stint at David C. Cook publishing company. Later he expanded into Bible publishing at the International Bible Society (now Biblica), which took him to dozens of countries across Africa, Asia, Europe and Latin America.

But his most visible contributions have come in the books he has written; this one is his fiftieth. Ten of these have been solo projects, such as *Sinners in the Hands of an Angry Church* (Zondervan, 1997) and *Damage Control: How to Stop Making Jesus Look Bad* (Baker, 2006). The other forty have been collaborations with such voices as Brooklyn Tabernacle pastor Jim Cymbala (four titles, including *Fresh Wind, Fresh Fire*, which was named Christian Book of the Year 2000); Compassion International president Wess Stafford; Southern Baptist megachurch leader Steve Gaines; Hobby Lobby founder David Green; and missionary hostage survivor Gracia Burnham (*In the Presence of My Enemies*, which became a *New York Times* bestseller and won a Gold Medallion award from the Evangelical Christian Publishers Association).

He was also the general editor of *Every Man's Bible* (Tyndale), which continues to sell strongly since its debut in 2004. For a full list of his books as well as many of his articles, see www.deanmerrill.com.

Ever a student of Holy Spirit empowerment across the church spectrum, Merrill attended the five-day Azusa Street Centennial in Los Angeles in April 2006 and visited historic sites there. In service to the Pentecostal/Charismatic Churches of North America (PCCNA), he researched and wrote *Miracle Invasion*, a collection of 39 vignettes of spiritual gifts in action across the United States and Canada. He is an ordained minister with the Fellowship of Christian Assemblies, which gave him a lifetime achievement award in 2019.

He and his wife, Grace, live in Colorado Springs, Colorado. They are the parents of three married children and the grandparents of twelve (ten biological, two adopted).

A key Scripture for him, displayed prominently in his writing office, is what was written about a certain Old Testament king: "He sought his God and worked wholeheartedly. And so he prospered" (2 Chronicles 31:21).